ANARCHISM

EXPLORING WORLD GOVERNMENTS

ABDO
Publishing Company

ANARCHISM

by A. M. Buckley

Content Consultant
Dana Ward, professor,
Political Studies,
Pitzer College

CREDITS

Published by ABDO Publishing Company, 8000 West 78th Street, Edina, Minnesota 55439. Copyright © 2011 by Abdo Consulting Group, Inc. International copyrights reserved in all countries. No part of this book may be reproduced in any form without written permission from the publisher. The Essential Library™ is a trademark and logo of ABDO Publishing Company.

Printed in the United States of America,
North Mankato, Minnesota
112010
012011

 THIS BOOK CONTAINS AT LEAST 10% RECYCLED MATERIALS.

Editor: Holly Saari
Copy Editor: David Johnstone
Interior Design and Production: Becky Daum
Cover Design: Becky Daum

Photo Credits: Hektor Pustina/AP Images, cover, 2, 3; iStockphoto, 9, 85; Michael Dwyer/AP Images, 15; Nadar/Getty Images, 19; Library of Congress, 31, 38, 41, 63, 73, 83, 103, 107; George Grantham Bain Collection/Library of Congress, 49; Hulton Archive/Getty Images, 53; AP Images, 61, 115; Willie B. Thomas/iStockphoto, 75; HALEY/SIPA/AP Images, 95; Dimitri Messinis/AP Images, 119; Bertil Ericson/Scanpix/ AP Images, 130; Jean-Christophe Bott/Keystone/AP Images, 133; Greg Baker/AP Images, 143

Library of Congress Cataloging-in-Publication Data
Buckley, A. M., 1968-
  Anarchism / by A.M. Buckley.
    p. cm. -- (Exploring world governments)
  Includes bibliographical references.
  ISBN 978-1-61714-788-3
  1. Anarchism. 2. Anarchism--History. I. Title.
  HX833.B83 2011
  335'.83--dc22
                                        2010039861

Table of Contents

What Is Government?

In the earliest, simplest societies, government as we know it did not exist. Family or tribal elders made decisions, and their powers were limited. As civilizations grew, governments developed to organize societies and to protect them from outside threats. As societies have grown in complexity, so have the governments that organize them. In this way, organizing society has led to massive bureaucracies with many offices and roles.

As of 2010, there were more than 190 countries, each with its own government. Two governments may look very similar on paper even though political life inside those countries varies greatly. Every government is different because it is influenced by its country's history, culture, economics, geography, and even psychology.

Still, governments share some main roles. Today, a main function of governments is to protect citizens from outside threats. This has evolved into the vast arena of international relations, including military alliances and trade agreements. Governments also organize power in a society. However, how power is acquired—through elections, heredity, or force—varies, as does who exercises it—one person, a few, or many.

Ideally, governments balance the rights of individuals against the needs of the whole society. But who defines those needs? Is it leaders chosen by universal suffrage, or is it a single dictator who assumed power through force? How are individual rights protected? The answers to these questions distinguish one form of government from another.

Another role of government is preserving internal order—that is, order as defined by those in power. While keeping order might mean prosecuting violent criminals in a democracy, in a dictatorship, it could mean prosecuting dissenters. Governments also look out for the welfare of their citizens. All modern governments provide some form of social services, ranging from education to housing to health care.

Governments are often involved in their national economies. Involvement can run the full spectrum—from completely planning the economy to merely levying taxes and allowing a free market to operate. Governments also regulate the private lives of citizens—from issuing marriage licenses in a democracy to enforcing specific styles of dress in a theocracy.

While all governments have some characteristics in common, the world's governments take many forms and make decisions differently. How does a government decide what individual rights to give its citizens? How are laws enforced? What happens when laws are broken? The answers to such questions depend on the political system at hand. ⌘

What Is Anarchism?

Imagine a girl who is surfing the Internet and comes across an interesting article about her favorite book, or maybe she finds the perfect brownie recipe. She might stop, read the article or download the recipe, but she does not have to pay a fee or consult the authorities.

Perhaps a group of teenagers decides to start a Web site about their favorite band. They need to know something about computers to make the Web site, but once they design it and upload the content, it is available to the public. They do not need to ask anyone official because online

The capability for free research on the Internet is an anarchist principle.

content is generated, maintained, and shared by millions of people just like these teens. And once online, it is equally available to anyone with an Internet connection.

Many people, including teenagers, join online social networks. Friends can post pictures from picnics or pool parties, sports events or lazy Saturday afternoons. While parents and teachers can provide important guidelines to keep children and teens safe online, there is no overriding Internet authority to tell anyone what he or she can or cannot post. The Internet is a publicly owned resource that is used freely and voluntarily by anyone who accesses it.

When the founders of the Internet developed it in the mid-1960s, they were concerned with creating an electronic web of communication, not the rare and often misunderstood school of thought called anarchism. Yet, the Internet has quickly grown into the largest and most widespread anarchist community to date.

> "In short, anarchism means a condition of society where all men and women are free, and where all enjoy equally the benefits of an ordered and sensible life."[1]
>
> —Alexander Berkman, anarchist, activist, and author

Defining Anarchism

When most people think of anarchy, they generally do not imagine the ordered searches and information-packed Web sites of cyberspace. They probably do not think about freedom of expression, shared resources, or the natural growth and development of ideas, but these elements are what the primary theorists of anarchism had in mind when they developed the political theory more than a century ago.

Both terms, anarchy and anarchism, are often misunderstood as comprising chaos and lawlessness. The word *anarchy* is derived from the Greek language and means "no ruler."[2] Anarchy is an absence of government, and anarchism is the full political theory in which order, balance, and harmony are integral ideals. Anarchists simply believe government hinders, rather than helps, achieve a state of harmony. They believe that balance is achieved through the natural development of a free community, much like the Internet. Anarchist principles also include equal access by all to resources, freedom of expression, beliefs, and participation, and no hierarchy—no single person is better or higher than another. This sense of equality and openness is evident on the Internet. Anarchist thinkers also place a high value on creativity, pleasure, and leisure as important parts of life and liberty.

Anarchists oppose government and the logic of the common phrase "law and order." Instead of envisioning law as bringing order, anarchists see it as creating an environment of coercion where individuals must behave in mandated ways. Anarchists view law as negative. They do not see crime and violence as natural to humans but as cultivations by societal structures in which one person has vastly more resources and opportunities than another. Anarchists believe in the fundamental justice and morality of humans and insist that these qualities would allow order and harmony to prevail in a society without government.

Common Misconceptions about Anarchism

If one thinks of anarchists as punk rockers or bomb throwers, and not as engineers, scientists, or students, it might be hard to conceive of the Internet as an anarchist community. While punk and violent anarchists exist, neither solely characterizes anarchism.

Anarchism has played a role in the world's political history, but its full story is often unfamiliar. Instead, a collection of tales, some true but others false or exaggerated, tend to shape most people's definition of anarchism.

The history of anarchism is composed of the stories of individual thinkers and activists and groups of workers and artisans. It spreads throughout the world and dates from the 1840s through the early part of the twentieth century. But in spirit, the ideas that define anarchism began much earlier and continue to the present day.

A few possibilities help to explain why the

"Anarchism means literally a society without *arkhos*, that is to say, without a ruler. It does not mean a society without law, and therefore it does not mean a society without order."[3]

—*Herbert Read, anarchist, philosopher, and poet*

history of anarchism has so often been misrepresented or misunderstood. One of these is the double meaning of the word *anarchy*. On the one hand, it can be used to describe a failed state, a controversial term applied most consistently to developing nations experiencing violence and disorder. Examples in recent history include Sudan and the Ivory Coast.

Another reason for anarchism's misrepresentation involves governments' influence on how history is told. If anarchists are opposed to the state, or the political organization of a sovereign territory, governments and governmental organizations are generally against anarchism. Because governments tend to define history and culture, officially sanctioned histories have the tendency to present information about anarchism that is skewed to one side: its most violent and revolutionary proponents are infamous, while its humanistic, idealistic, and egalitarian vision of society is often overlooked.

Challenging Assumptions

However, several sources relay the full scope of anarchism. In 1980, historian Howard Zinn wrote a book of history that was unlike any other before it. Rather than following the traditional point of view of events in history, *A People's History of the United States: 1492–present* presents history from the point of view of those who had been left out of prior histories. Zinn began by looking at the colonization of the Americas from the perspective of Native Americans and proceeded to examine the civil rights movement and other important chapters in US history from the point of view of people whose voices had been unheard or subdued.

In his book, Zinn, an anarchist, tried to reveal the sides of history that are often overshadowed. He did this as well with anarchism by writing introductions to at least two books about anarchism and a foreword to *The Alexander Berkman Reader*, a book compiling the writings of the important Russian-American anarchist. Zinn made the point that, during his many years of studying history throughout college and graduate school, he had never heard of Alexander Berkman. In light of this, Zinn explained,

> To bring Berkman to public attention is to present to all of us, and especially to a new generation of young people looking for guidance in a chaotic world, an inspiring example of living an honest life, as well as a vision of a better society.[4]

Besides being a historian, Howard Zinn was also a playwright and a social activist.

In his historical writings, Zinn indicated the importance of new perspectives. If one looks at anarchists with the certainty that they are thieves and thugs, one will see a band of criminals. From a certain point of view, the same could be said about those who commit officially sanctioned violence, such as soldiers who fight a war declared by their government.

How Can Anarchism Be Achieved?

Most anarchists share a common set of ideals, but they do not all agree on what anarchism is and how it should be achieved. Because of this, anarchism, like the Internet, is complex and diverse. There are many voices and points of view.

Historically, anarchists have been idealists who imagine a society without any form of authority forcing people to act one way or another. The society anarchists envision differs greatly from what is practiced in the vast majority of the world today. Because of that, anarchists do not advocate for small-scale change—like shifting from one government to another or protecting one aspect of the environment at a time—but large-scale change. To achieve an anarchist society today would necessitate changing the attitudes of billions of people, changing society's deeply conditioned reliance on authority, and adapting humans' relationships to each other and the shared world. Throughout

"The word *anarchy* unsettles most people in the Western world; it suggests disorder, violence, uncertainty. We have good reason to fear these conditions, because we have been living with them for a long time, not in anarchist societies (there have never been any) but exactly those societies fearful of anarchy—the powerful nation-states of modern times."[5]

—*Howard Zinn, historian and professor*

history, some anarchists have advocated this change through violence, while others have advocated for a peaceful revolution.

Anarchists state that humans can govern themselves, can live in equality and harmony with each other and with the environment, and can share the earth's riches freely—all without governmental intervention. Rather than seeking answers in authority or government, anarchists ask people to rely on their own goodwill, responsibility, and ideas. The aspiration may sound like a fictional utopia, but anarchists insist it is a dream that can be reality. ⌘

Early History of Anarchism

Anarchism did not emerge as a movement until the mid-nineteenth century, yet its ideas have roots in earlier times. Throughout history, people have sought to find a balance between individual freedom and overriding authority.

Intellectual Forerunners

A significant number of individuals have written about or practiced ideas central to anarchism throughout the centuries. In ancient China, the writings of Lao-tzu, widely considered to be the

One of the founders of anarchism, Mikhail Bakunin believed government was a form of oppression.

father of Taoism, have been cited as a precursor to anarchism. Lao-tzu emphasized the natural unfolding of events—much like anarchists who value natural growth—and living in balance with nature as central to human happiness.

For centuries in India, *sadhus*, or holy men, have left organized society to pursue their faith. In most cases, they shun personal property and live off the land, dedicating their time to spiritual pursuits. Their absence of personal property and reliance on the earth are examples of anarchist thinking.

Perhaps the most direct precedent to anarchism is found in the ancient Greek philosopher Zeno. His writing emphasized individual morality and opposed the authority of government. Zeno stated that if all people were reasonable, no courts or police would be needed. Like the anarchists after him, Zeno had a strong belief in the moral capacity of humanity. Without the interference of government, he believed people would thrive, with time for work, leisure, artistic interests, and spiritual pursuits not necessarily based on organized religion.

Communal Living

All over the world and throughout history, societies have organized themselves in the kinds of communal groups that anarchists promote in place of governmental authority. People who live communally share resources and property instead of having private property. In North America, Australia, and Africa, for example, people have lived together in different types of interdependent tribes, bands, or clans. In medieval Europe, craftspeople organized themselves into independent guilds that provided protection and mutual support. In England, from 1649 to 1650, a group of peasant farmers called Diggers took over a plot of public land in order to grow food for themselves and their families. Anarchists' admiration of the communal lifestyles of many primitive societies has led some critics to call anarchists backward-thinking or against progress.

Enlightened Thinkers

During the eighteenth century, scholars of the Enlightenment, also called the age of reason, wrote and spoke out against the Christian church, the pervasive authority at the time, in favor of thought and reason. Enlightenment philosophers were not anarchists or even, in most cases, revolutionaries. But early anarchist thinkers found inspiration in Enlightenment philosophers' belief that human reason took precedence over submission to authority—religious or governmental. Enlightenment thinkers also spoke out against the corrupting nature of progress, specifically the rise of industry and modern cities, on human morality.

One of the Enlightenment thinkers was Jean-Jacques Rousseau, a Swiss philosopher who lived and worked in France in the eighteenth century. Rousseau valued the senses alongside reason and emphasized the importance of individuality, embracing personal choice and responsibility over institutional mandates. Like Zeno, Rousseau believed in the basic goodness of humankind and blamed injustice not on individuals but on poorly organized governments. Rousseau's alternative was democracy, not anarchism, and his ideas helped shape modern democracy. Still, his idea that any government would soon decrease the benefit of community life influenced anarchists.

Stirrings of Discontent

Though not given the name anarchism, the political and economic ideas of the theory of anarchism were first laid out in *Enquiry Concerning Political Justice,* written by William Godwin in 1793. The book, which sold many copies at the time, asserts that laws do not derive from the leaders' goodness or wisdom but from their ambition and passion; therefore, these laws lead to injustice and corruption rather than to the justice they espouse. A fairer system, he believed, would be to select individuals to decide on supposed crimes or illegal actions.

Godwin promoted the abolition of government. As an idealist and a humanist, he maintained that people, if left to their own without interference, would be orderly and peaceful. Like many anarchists, Godwin was initially against individual property, arguing that resources should be divided according to need and desire, an idea that is common to most forms of anarchism.

Godwin's belief that economy should be based on the community's shared needs and the Enlightenment philosophers' advocacy of reason over authority relate as much to anarchism as to two important bodies of economic and political thought that developed at the same time, socialism and communism. The interaction, overlap, and, at times, competition among these has continued throughout anarchism's history.

The Founders of Anarchism

The first person to use the word *anarchy* to describe his ideas about society was Frenchman Pierre-Joseph Proudhon in his book *What is Property?*, written in 1840. Proudhon answers his own question simply: "Property is theft."[1] This revolutionary idea would be embraced by subsequent anarchists, most profoundly by Proudhon's friend and follower Mikhail Bakunin, with whom Proudhon shares a legacy as the founder of anarchism. But taken in the context of his body of work, what Proudhon opposed was when a few people own the resources needed by many. He perceived this as one person exercising authority over another.

Anarchism, by definition, respects individual points of view. Within its guiding principles there

ANARCHISM IN LATIN AMERICA

Anarchism was transplanted to Latin America along with socialism and communism during the 1880s. Anarchist ideas took root in Argentina, Mexico, and Chile. The idea of autonomous and interdependent communities resonated with indigenous people and mirrored the ancient ways of life of the Aztecs and Incas.

is room for differing opinions. For example, the lifelong friends and founders shared the goal of abolishing the state, or political institutions, but disagreed about how to achieve this. Their biographies also differ; Proudhon came from poverty and remained connected to his roots as an artisan and worker throughout his life. Bakunin was the son of a noble Russian family.

Perhaps the most significant difference between these two founders is the way they perceived change. While Proudhon believed in a gradual, nonviolent shift in power from authority to the people, Bakunin was a passionate revolutionary who believed violence was necessary for change. The two represent very different sides of anarchism. Though Bakunin's ideas would predominate for many decades, more recent history has shown a return to Proudhon's sense of gradual and peaceful revolution. In one of few detailed histories of anarchism, author and scholar Richard Sonn observed,

> That anarchism could claim as its founders two such contrasting figures as Pierre-Joseph Proudhon and Mikhail Bakunin says a great deal about the lack of doctrinal orthodoxy required of adherents to the movement.[2]

The Early Days

Proudhon was very much inspired by Rousseau and shared his belief in the morality of humankind. He agreed with Rousseau's critique of modernization and its effect on morality but vehemently disagreed with the remedies

Rousseau laid out in his book *Social Contract*. According to Proudhon, Rousseau left economics out of the solution. Proudhon, chiefly dedicated to the rights of workers and artisans, believed that control over one's own work and material was vital to achieving liberty and social reform. In his view, ownership of watches, clothing, chairs, and other fruits of labor was key to artisans' and workers' freedom. Proudhon was strongly opposed to the accumulation of resources by a few. He advocated for banks that offered credit, or the amount of money a person can use, for free instead of being charged interest. He also advocated for banks that would also allow for the free exchange of goods and services in place of money.

In Proudhon's view, change would come over time as people organized themselves into mutually supportive coalitions and owned the means of production, or the materials and tools necessary for work. In this way, they would reorder the economy and eventually establish a system free of exploitation. In later books, Proudhon outlined a similar plan for land in which autonomous societies would coexist without authority and trade openly with one another. Proudhon outlined his ideas in 26 books and voluminous correspondence and actively worked to limit exploitation however he could.

In 1848, laborers elected Proudhon to serve in the National Assembly, France's legislative body. He did so, despite his opposition to the idea of government the assembly represented, and he used his seat to support workers' rights.

He was unpopular with other officials in the assembly. At one point he proposed a bill to impose a rental tax in order to create funds for free credit. Of the 695 ballots cast, it received only two votes, one of them being Proudhon's. Not long afterward, Proudhon wrote a scathing critique of the newly elected president, Napoléon III, and was imprisoned for three years.

Like Proudhon, Bakunin was jailed for his anarchist beliefs and spent time in a desolate Siberian cell before his escape in 1861. Before his imprisonment, Bakunin studied philosophy and was interested in revolution. But in the years after his imprisonment, Bakunin became an anarchist.

Bakunin followed his friend and mentor Proudhon's ideas closely, with two notable exceptions: property and methodology. Bakunin insisted that all property was anathema, or basically a curse, to liberty and that materials and products were co-owned by everyone in society. Also, unlike his contemporary, Bakunin was open to violence as a method for change.

In 1844, approximately 15 years before defining himself as an anarchist, Bakunin wrote, "The passion to destroy is a creative passion."[3] This incendiary idea would come to identify much of his work with and influence on anarchism.

Workers Unite

In 1864, a group of workers from several European countries, including France, Germany, England, Ireland, Poland, and Italy, founded the

International Working Men's Association, also called First International, to empower laborers to find ways to free themselves from economic oppression. Anarchists were deeply involved in the founding of the association, and the majority of its early members favored Proudhon's economic policies. But by the time the organization got underway, the peaceful anarchist founder was ill, and he died a year later.

Bakunin and Marx

Bakunin's economic views were similar to those of his contemporary, Karl Marx, the founder of communism. Bakunin and Marx were founding members of the First International and figured prominently in its history. The two struggled over leadership of the association for several years and engaged in a bitter rivalry throughout their lives.

The feud between Bakunin and Marx is puzzling to some historians. In an article exploring their relationship, contemporary scholar Ann Robertson wrote,

> Convinced that capitalism is predicated on the exploitation of workers by capitalists, [Bakunin and Marx] were equally dedicated to fighting for a socialist society where economic classes would be abolished and all individuals would have the opportunity to develop all of their creative capacities.[4]

Similarly, they agreed that freedom would not be won easily and that a revolution was necessary. Roberts continued,

Finally, they agreed that the State was an instrument of class oppression, not some neutral organ that equitably represented everyone's interests, and in the final analysis must be abolished.[5]

It is probably true that a clash of personalities played into their power struggle. The fervently antiauthoritarian Bakunin saw in Marx yet another version of a dictator, and Marx seemed to see Bakunin as a radical and a conspirator. In 1871, at the end of the Franco-German War, the First International began to split along ideological lines. Under Marx's leadership, the German workers sought ways to function with the system. Bakunin, on the other hand, maintained that abolishing the state was the only way to achieve real change. Some of the workers, predominantly in Spain, Italy, Switzerland, and Belgium, agreed with Bakunin's plan. They split off from the main body of the First International and formed their own sect of the association with Bakunin as their moral and ideological leader.

> "The government of man by man is servitude."[6]
>
> —Pierre-Joseph Proudhon, the father of anarchism

Guided by Bakunin, they acted on the belief that no single person was free until all were free. They sought liberation from authority and total communal ownership of the means and results of their work. In the time leading up to the split, adversaries of the dissenting workers had referred to them as anarchists. Now these workers proudly took the name as their own.

The split in the First International fed the growing feud between Marx and Bakunin. In 1872, Marx found reason to expel Bakunin from the group. Bakunin and the other anarchists soon formed their own association, which was success-ful in working for labor causes for a short-lived period. ⌘

3

The Heyday Part One: Anarchism and Violence

The period from approximately 1880 until the time of World War I (1914–1918) is known as the heyday of anarchism, a short-lived and stormy time when anarchists were active in many parts of the world. During the anarchist heyday, much of the world was changing. What many called the second Industrial Revolution was occurring—transportation and communications systems experienced explosive growth. Effects of the first Industrial Revolution, when factories,

Peter Kropotkin became an important anarchist leader in the late nineteenth century.

regimentation, and an emphasis on production values and profit margins became increasingly important, could still be felt in communities. Also, the world was transforming from a structure of small municipalities toward one made up of large nation-states. Aided by the Enlightenment philosophers' challenge to the pervasive power of the church, science gained popularity and continued to fuel industry and technology.

These historic changes threatened core anarchist principles of freedom, natural development and growth, and autonomous, local communities. Perhaps this also explains the relative popularity of anarchism during this time; as the world changed, some people who were invested in individual liberties and social equality clung to anarchism as a last hope.

Anarchism usually spread in regions and among people left out of the blur of industrial changes. Rural communities of farmers and artisans, enclaves of artists and poets, and outsiders—sometimes criminals—flocked to the freedom and creative potential promised by anarchism. However, anarchism still took hold in some industrialized areas.

A New Leader Emerges

By the time of his death in 1876, Bakunin had taken anarchism in a new and increasingly volatile direction. As the heyday began, anarchists found another visionary leader in the unlikely figure of a Russian prince. Peter Kropotkin was the third important anarchist leader and remained active during anarchism's heyday.

Kropotkin's background influenced his involvement in anarchism. Born into Russian royalty in 1842, he studied to become a geographer. As a young man, he was sent to Siberia as a member of the army to study the region and its population. There, he was greatly influenced by the communal values, cultural diversity, and cooperation he witnessed among the different Siberian tribes. Returning home to Russia, he was dismayed to find that the time of progressive change had given way to centralized government.

Kropotkin took a government position with little responsibility so he could devote time to working for the Russian Royal Geographical Society. In 1871, he traveled to Switzerland for the society, where he came into contact with, and soon joined, the anarchist movement. Upon his return to Russia, he began speaking out for social reform. Like the two primary anarchist leaders before him, Kropotkin was jailed for his efforts to bring change. But after two years in prison, he escaped in 1876.

Kropotkin left Russia for Western Europe. He wrote extensively about anarchism and actively participated in the movement. In Geneva, Switzerland, in 1879, Kropotkin helped to found *Le Révolté*, which later moved to Paris under the name *La Révolte*, a leading anarchist publication. During the 1880s, he was imprisoned again as one of many anarchists rounded up and jailed. After his release, he moved to England, where he lived quietly for many years, writing extensively about anarchist ideas. In his work and writings, Kropotkin, a trained scientist, grounded anarchism's ideals and principles in the vocabulary and from the perspective of science.

Propaganda by the Deed

Anarchists and other radicals responded to the development of large-scale industry and centralized governments in a variety of ways. In Italy, a prominent anarchist named Errico Malatesta had attempted a violent insurgency, but he failed to overthrow the government. In Russia, a group of reformist revolutionaries—not associated with anarchists—assassinated the Russian czar, Alexander II.

In light of these events, a group of anarchists held a meeting and adopted a course of action that would define them for decades. Anarchist historian Richard Sonn wrote of the period,

> Strongly influenced by this revolutionary success [in Russia], the anarchists at the congress, including Kropotkin, recommended the

doctrine known as propaganda by the deed as an efficacious way of spreading the spirit of revolt among the people.[1]

By this, they allowed violence to be used as one way to promote their ideals and make way for change. Propaganda by the deed meant forwarding anarchism's ideas by taking action and not just speaking about them. Kropotkin, not a fiery extremist, first agreed with the principle, but later regretted his association with anarchist violence.

Over the next three decades, anarchists resorted to violence in areas around the world. Some of these were individual acts of violence intended to avenge the deaths of other anarchists at the hands of authorities. Other violent acts were intended to bring attention to their cause—propaganda of the deed in action. And still other acts of violence were deemed necessary in order to make way for the kind of extreme social change anarchists believed was necessary. It is doubtful that the peaceful Proudhon would have approved of this course of action. Despite many pacifist anarchists, both historical and contemporary, and anarchists' humanistic aims, anarchism has been unable to shake the violence associated with this time period.

Violence at Haymarket Square

As anarchists became more organized in Europe and the Americas, their demands for work reform had greater impact. At the time, people worked much longer hours in factories, and workers' demands centered on the hotly contested workday. Labor unions, supported by anarchists and others, wanted to institute an eight-hour workday, while factory owners did not.

The debate over the workday came to a head in Chicago, Illinois, on May 1, 1886. Groups of workers of various politics, including unionists, socialists, and anarchists, joined together to protest in favor of the eight-hour workday. For a week, workers held meetings and led marches. On May 1, approximately 35,000 workers throughout the United States went on strike. In the days that followed, tens of thousands more workers joined them. Police clashed with strikers, sometimes violently, killing at least two.

Anarchists organized a meeting and called for revenge. The mayor attended the meeting, held at Haymarket Square, and asked police not to intervene. Nevertheless, police found cause to disperse the workers. During the tussle, someone threw a bomb that immediately killed a police officer. Violence ensued, and seven police officers and an untold number of workers were killed.

In the days after the tragedy at Haymarket Square, hundreds of people were arrested. Despite the fact that the bomb thrower's identity and politics were unknown, eight leading anarchists were tried and convicted of murder. Although some were not even in Haymarket Square, their criticism of corporations and capitalism was alleged to have inspired the bomb. As the *Encyclopedia of Chicago* states,

Lacking credible evidence that the defendants threw the bomb or organized the bomb throwing, prosecutors focused on their writings and speeches. The jury, instructed to adopt a conspiracy theory without legal precedent, convicted all eight. Seven were sentenced to death.[2]

The results of the trial were publicized worldwide, and, as the encyclopedic entry continues, "The trial is now considered one of the worst miscarriages of justice in American history."[3] Of those sentenced, one committed suicide in his cell, four were hanged, and the governor later pardoned the remaining three.

Workers' attempts to establish an eight-hour workday in the United States inspired more workers in Europe, Russia, and other parts of the world to lobby for fairer conditions. As a result of the Haymarket bomb trial, the first of May was named May Day and is a workers' holiday in several countries.

Tumultuous Times

In the following years, anarchists were increasingly sidelined in the United States and Europe by government and socialist reformers. In 1889, three years after the Haymarket trial, a new workers' foundation, the Second Socialist International, was formed, but anarchists were denied entry. As anarchist leaders sought to maintain a platform, violence and retribution by anarchists and social reformers continued to mar anarchist reputation.

THE CHICAGO ANARCHISTS OF 1886.

looked worse
the defense-
Dozens who
slight shot-
ened away,
ts which were
1. The gang,
ed upon the
women and
away the se-
ded. How
ally injured,
y were mor-
, could not be
ith certainty,
we are not
n we place
of mortally
bout six, and
injured at
We know of
whom was
leen, another
d, another in
and another
1. A dying
Doedick, was
e on an ex-
y two police-
ople did not
g boy. They
two murder-
the rascals'

Attention Workingmen!

GREAT

MASS-MEETING

TO-NIGHT, at 7.30 o'clock,

AT THE

HAYMARKET, Randolph St., Bet. Desplaines and Halsted.

Good Speakers will be present to denounce the latest
atrocious act of the police, the shooting of our
fellow-workmen yesterday afternoon.

Workingmen Arm Yourselves and Appear in Full Force!

THE EXECUTIVE COMMITTEE

Achtung, Arbeiter!

Große

Massen-Versammlung

Heute Abend, ½8 Uhr, auf dem

Heumarkt Randolph-Straße, zwischen

The meeting at Haymarket Square was advertised in an anarchist newspaper in 1886.

Anarchists continued to join workers' strikes and sign up workers in unions in the United States, Europe, and, increasingly, Latin America. They gained attention through organizing as well as through acts of violence. Trials and punishments that many perceived as unjust, such as the Haymarket trial, brought more attention to anarchism.

Global Violence

Soon, anarchist violence escalated across the globe. In Paris, France, in 1892, anarchist Francois Ravachol attempted to kill a judge and a prosecutor with a bomb. Another bombing occurred after that, killing a restaurant owner suspected of informing on Ravachol. In Spain, anarchists continued to organize and resist the status quo, and scores of them were rounded up and executed. In 1894, an Italian anarchist assassinated President Carnot of France, seeking to avenge the death of a French anarchist whom the government had executed. In 1897, anarchist Michele Angiolillo shot and killed the prime minister of Spain, a country known to have tortured anarchists.

As individual anarchists acted out against the authorities, retribution against anarchists escalated in the form of political roundups and violent crackdowns on workers' protests as well as imprisonment, torture, or execution for suspected crimes. In the framework of history, the acts of terror committed by anarchists did little to further their cause. ⌘

ASSASSINATION BY AN ANARCHIST

On September 6, 1901, Leon Czolgosz, a Detroit-born, self-declared anarchist of Polish parents, shot President William McKinley of the United States. McKinley died of his wounds on September 14. After a quick trial, Czolgosz was found guilty and sentenced to death. He was electrocuted in a New York State prison on October 29.

4

The Heyday Part Two: Anarchism and Society

Ine of anarchists' prevailing claims is that their ideas are not mere theory or fantasy but are in fact real ways of living and thinking. As a result, many anarchists value direct action in favor of just writing about, theorizing about, or discussing anarchism's possibilities. Yet, because anarchists oppose hierarchy, organizing anarchists to act has proven difficult. In his history of anarchism, Richard Sonn wrote, "Anarchists were notoriously difficult to organize. Anarchists

always idealized the federation of autonomous groups who made joint decision on a voluntary basis."[1] The question arose: how could anarchists, who resisted authority, organize themselves as opposed to having their society and economics organized by the state?

One way they attempted to organize was through international meetings or councils, but not everyone agreed, and all opinions were considered to be valid. For example, although propaganda by the deed was established as a precedent at one conference, not all anarchists agreed with its violent interpretation. Like his predecessor, Proudhon, influential German anarchist Gustav Landauer was a lifelong pacifist, and the well-known American anarchist Emma Goldman was quoted in the *Chicago Tribune* as saying succinctly, "An anarchist who believes in division of property, the killing of the rich, and the burning of fine houses is an idiot."[2]

Workers Unite in Syndicates

After a wave of violence and political assassinations in the early twentieth century, anarchists again attempted to find a way to organize. The primary form of organization to emerge at this point was syndicalism. The system is similar to organizing by labor unions: syndicates, or small groups of independent workers, each maintain control of their work and cooperate voluntarily with the other syndicates.

In 1906 and 1907, anarchists meeting in Europe supported the continued use of syndicalism to free workers from governmental and capitalist intervention and exploitation. Although all did not agree, the majority favored the continued use of syndicalism as a way to move toward more equality and worker control.

During the early twentieth century, anarchists led hundreds of thousands of workers to trade unions, more than at any other time in history. In fact, anarchists joined the International Workers of the World in the United States in large numbers. Syndicalism was so popular that anarchism and syndicalism became nearly synonymous. It empowered workers to defend their interests collectively, and in the end, the goal to revolutionize society remained.

Integral Education

In addition to economics, anarchists addressed the needs of the younger generation. The anarchist approach to teaching and learning was called integral education and has had perhaps the largest single effect on contemporary society of any anarchist idea. Though theorists as early as Proudhon had discussed the idea, the individual most closely associated with integral education is Spanish anarchist and educator Francisco Ferrer. To this day, Ferrer's philosophies remain pivotal to educational theory and practice.

In line with anarchism's insistence on individual freedom and creativity, integral education values a child's interests and skills. Integral education is informed by the Socratic method, a style of education based on the Greek philosopher Socrates, which emphasizes questions over answers. As students of integral education express curiosity, educators pose questions to help them find answers. Integral education is a process of learning through exploration rather than having knowledge passed down to students by their teachers. Experience is also an important part of integral education. In addition to learning from books, classes take many field trips and excursions. In some cases, students also learn a trade. A balance of practical and theoretical knowledge is vital to integral education.

Ferrer was born in Barcelona in 1859. He lived for a time in Paris and, after developing his ideas about education, returned to Spain to open the Escuela Moderna, or the Modern School. The school included adult education and became a center for anarchist activities. Ferrer's methods were so popular that by 1905 there were 14 similar schools in Barcelona and 34 more throughout Spain; all were based on his model of education.

But Ferrer would not escape the wave of violence that surrounded anarchism during the time period. In 1909, authorities executed him after a violent anarchist uprising. He was never convicted of being involved in the protest, and people around the world demonstrated against what they saw as the unjust killing of the educator.

The Ferrer Center

Ferrer's ideas about education spread throughout the world. Free schools based on his model opened in countries such as the United States,

Argentina, and China. Ferrer not only informed anarchist schools, but his methods are still cited by progressive educators today.

American anarchist Emma Goldman, who had immigrated to North America from Lithuania at the age of 16, helped to establish the Ferrer Association in the United States. Goldman, together with prominent anarchists, including Russian expatriate Alexander Berkman, were members of the first Modern School—founded by Alexis and Elizabeth Byrne Ferm, Leonard Abbot, Joseph Ishill, and Harry Kelly—in New York City in 1911. Named the Ferrer Center, the school was a vibrant and progressive educational center and attracted scores of artists, philosophers, educators, and writers and was a center of artistic energy and political activity. It offered classes and workshops in theater, art, feminism, politics, and history. Artists Robert Henri and George Bellows taught classes there, and surreal artist Man Ray was a regular at the center. Feminists Margaret Sanger and Helen Gurley Brown

INTEGRAL EDUCATION IN FRANCE

In 1904, French anarchist Sebastien Faure opened a school outside Paris. Twenty to 40 boys and girls lived and studied at the school, La Ruche, or The Hive. Until age 12, they attended classes. After that, they studied and participated in the life of the community by working on the land or in workshops. The Hive was distinct from strict schools run by the church or the state; teachers emphasized students' own ideas and autonomy.

gave lectures along with others in the anarchist community, including Voltarine de Cleyre, Saja-Kichi Hartmann, Will Durant, Charles Sprading, Hippolyte Ravel, and Becky Edelsohn.

In 1914, a bomb went off in the home of Louise Berger, one of the anarchists involved with the Ferrer Center, killing Berger and three others. It was allegedly intended for the industrialist John D. Rockefeller. The explosion incited a series of investigations and raids on anarchists by the authorities. As a result, the Ferrer Center moved to New Jersey and was renamed the Ferrer Colony and Modern School.

Women's Rights

Anarchists' values of freedom and individual liberty are not limited to work and education; they extend to family life and women. But not all anarchists agree on what this means.

During the nineteenth century, when Proud-hon was still living and writing, some anarchists promoted what was called free love. At that time, free love meant having the freedom to begin and end relationships whenever mutually agreed upon. This, at a time when divorce was taboo, was considered radical. But Proudhon, the primary anarchist thinker in the movement's early days, held to traditional ideas about marriage and family. It is paradoxical that he believed so wholeheartedly in individual freedom but did not extend his thinking to women's rights.

In fact, women's rights are little mentioned throughout anarchist history, with only a few notable exceptions. Spanish anarchist Federica Montseny, who was born to anarchist intellectuals in 1905 and died in 1994, spent most of her life working for equal rights for women. She argued that a complete social revolution was impossible without women being accepted as equals. As a young woman, she wrote articles and novels emphasizing the struggles of Spanish women. She urged women not to aim to act or dress like men, but to strive for equality as humans.

> "I believe that when two people love each other that no judge, minister or court, or body of people have anything to do with it. They themselves are the ones to determine the relations that they shall hold with one another. When that relation becomes irksome to either party, or one of the parties, then it can be as quietly terminated as it was formed."[3]
>
> —Emma Goldman, anarchist, activist, and writer

Health Care

Like other resources, anarchists determined that all should share health care equally. Similar to a Communist approach to work, doctors' abilities were valued equally with those of teachers, electricians, and trash collectors. In *The ABC of Anarchism*, Alexander Berkman wrote that it is impossible to place a value on the work of a surgeon or a carpenter or anyone else. If it takes the same amount of time to save a life and fix a car, would the surgeon still be paid more? But what if the car being fixed were taking the surgeon to the hospital? Posing questions such as these helped Berkman explain his ideas. They also help philosophers considering anarchism work toward the idea of job equality.

Historically, anarchists' primary contribution to health care has been by women. Montseny, in Spain, who briefly held a government position as Minister of Health, worked to gain equal health care for all, including women and the poor. Among her achievements in this area were the implementation of family planning, birth control, and legalized abortion, which shocked the traditionally Catholic country. Equally indicative of her influence, Montseny was the first woman to hold a governmental position in Spain, and she did this as an anarchist.

CHINESE FEMINIST AND ANARCHIST

In the early twentieth century, Chinese feminist and anarchist He Zhen spoke out against the cultural practices of foot binding and polygamy that she saw as harmful to women. He also thought women should be liberated from the patriarchal family system.

In the United States, Goldman, who was trained as a nurse, worked for equality and accessibility to health care for women and the poor. Long before it was socially acceptable—it was even illegal at the time—Goldman advocated for birth control for women. Feminists were invited to the Ferrer Center to speak out about how birth control could give women more freedom in exercising control over their reproductive systems.

In 1914, a crowd gathered in Union Square in New York City to hear anarchist Alexander Berkman speak.

Backlash and Deportations

The heyday of anarchism ended with the advent of World War I in 1914. In the decades leading up to it, anarchists, though still a small minority worldwide, had been active in many countries. They established community centers and equity stores—stores that offer goods for trade of other goods or services—unions and syndicates, Modern Schools, and progressive newspapers. But they also assassinated world leaders and heads of corporations. As the world moved toward war, there was less room for their dissenting voices.

The United States passed a law in 1903 that banned anarchists from entering the country. Once the war began, the government tried to deport anarchists and other liberal intellectuals. In 1919, Goldman and Berkman were among those deported for their political and social views and activities. They initially went to Russia, but, disillusioned by the revolution there, they moved to other countries.

In Germany, the government executed anarchists and liberal writers and thinkers. In perhaps one of the more ironic tragedies to befall anarchists at the time, German anarchist and philosopher Gustav Landauer, a lifelong pacifist, was beaten to death by German authorities in 1919.

Russia initially provided hope for progressive socialism, if not anarchism. The Bolsheviks, a small minority of revolutionaries who organized into workers' councils, successfully overthrew the czar in 1917. But hope soured during the ensuing Russian Revolution when Vladimir Lenin,

CONTESTED GUILT

In May 1920, Nicola Sacco and Bartolomeo Vanzetti, Italian-American anarchists, were arrested on suspicion of robbery. It was widely believed that the two were not guilty but had fallen into a police trap. An attorney who had represented many clients in labor suits, Fred H. Moore, defended them. In what grew into one of the most highly publicized and hotly contested trials in history, the two men were eventu-ally convicted and sentenced to death. During the course of the trial, the men captured the hearts and spirits of people around the world. In August 1927, after a lengthy trial and international public demonstrations on their behalf, Sacco and Vanzetti were executed by the state of Massachusetts, where they had been tried.

a disciple of Marx, vied for Bolshevik power. Disillusionment continued in the following totalitarian regime of Joseph Stalin.

Although World War I did not signal the complete end of anarchism—the movement made significant gains during and after the war, first in Ukraine, and then in Spain—the time period certainly marked the beginning of the end of anarchism for several years. ⌘

US ARRESTS AND RELEASES

In 1918, a small group of Jewish Russian-Americans published a Yiddish anarchist newspaper called *Frayhayt*, defending the Russian Revolution and opposing US intervention. Most were arrested for distributing the paper, and one member, Jacob Schwartz, died in custody after a police beating. To free their comrades, members formed the Political Prisoners Defense Committee. As a result, members Jack Abrams, Mollie Steiner, Sam Lipman, and Hyman Lachowsky were freed and deported to Russia in 1921.

5

Poetry, Protest, and Punks

World War I had split many anarchists upon ideological lines. Kropotkin had supported the Allies in the war effort, and a great number of anarchists strongly disagreed with his position, citing anarchism's lack of support for any government or coercive action. Deeply disappointed, many anarchists lost faith in their philosophical leader. This split came at a time when the already loose ranks of anarchists were in further disarray due to clashes with government and police, deportations, and their

During the 1950s, writer Herbert Read brought anarchist principles to a new generation.

own sullied reputation due to violence against heads of state and business.

World War I ended in 1918 and was followed not long afterward by the Great Depression (1929–1933), a period of worldwide economic strain. Anarchist activity had decreased or been silenced in most parts of the world, but it thrived briefly in Ukraine under the leadership of peasant anarchist Nestor Makhno and for a longer period of time in Spain, where anarchist syndicates and communes held out against the government in the decades preceding the Spanish Civil War. Even in Spain, where anarchists experienced their greatest and lengthiest success, the movement ended in 1939 with the civil war victory of General Francisco Franco's forces, aided by the fascist governments of Italy and Germany.

Lone Voice for Reason

By the mid-twentieth century, anarchism's primary leaders had passed away, and anarchism's popularity dwindled. However, one writer continued to expand the ideas of anarchism. In the largely quiet 1950s, English anarchist, critic, and poet Herbert Read wrote the essays that comprise *Anarchy and Order*.

In his essays, Read made a strong case for the reconsideration of anarchism. In particular, he focused on anarchism's idealistic and holistic embrace of art, the imagination, and spirituality as essential to human freedom. In a climate of growing commercialism, Read saw the culture of the day as bankrupt and desperately in need of change. His view of the world was colored by the times. The Great Depression and the rise of totalitarian regimes had culminated in World War II (1939–1944), while democracies in the United States and Western Europe fueled the growth of capitalism. Read's ideas grew out of his study of anarchism as much as his growing disillusionment with what he perceived as a placid and superficial culture of consumption.

Read outlined the principles of anarchism for a contemporary audience, since the movement was at least three decades beyond its peak. He looked back on anarchist activities with some historical distance and contrasted anarchism's heyday with the simultaneous rise of socialism, communism, and fascism. But as a twentieth-century philosopher and poet, Read also wrote about anarchism in relation to capitalism and the formulation of nation-states with centralized authority and bureaucracy. His writings offered anarchism as a more holistic alternative to stubborn bureaucracies.

As optimistic as he was about anarchism, Read was equally negative in his assessment of art and culture in the wake of the Industrial Revolution. The 1950s were a time of relative prosperity, and though Read did not wish to turn back the clock, he bemoaned individuals' lack of opportunity to reason and to reflect, rather than to accept blindly what was offered for consumption.

Read placed the blame for the superficiality and emptiness of culture on the social system. He wrote, "The ordinary man under our present unjust system has to have his education stopped before his mind is fully opened." He also added, "From the age of fourteen, he is caught up in an endless treadmill."[1] What Read saw in his home of England and in other Western societies, including the United States, was a deep attachment to work and money and a lack of interest in art, philosophy, or culture. For Read, this constituted a different form of enslavement, not to a ruler, but to production and consumption.

More Anticapitalist Writing

An artist and philosopher in France expanded on the idea that capitalism produced cultural malaise. In 1957, Guy Debord was one of the original founders of an artistic and social group called the Situationist International. Though they did not identify as anarchists, the Situationists looked to both anarchist history and recent art history for inspiration. The Situationists saw art as integral to social progress and capitalism as destructive of creativity and imagination.

Like Read had done, the Situationists saw capitalism as dividing people into categories: producers and consumers. But they added the terms of actors and spectators. Debord expanded on these ideas in *Society of the Spectacle*, published in 1967. In this book, he defines *spectacle* as the onslaught of images produced in a capitalist society and posed that these comprised a new kind of authoritative power. For Debord, people were trapped in a web of images as coercive as government was to earlier anarchists.

Like the anarchists before him, Debord, whose writings expressed anarchist tendencies, attacked all forms of hierarchy, including the system of wage-labor, or being paid money for work. He argued that capitalism produced false needs and reduced the unique individual to a consumer fulfilling those needs. Though not widely recognized during his lifetime, Debord's book influenced student protestors in France. In Paris in 1968, students rebelled against what they perceived as an overcrowded and outdated university system. They wanted greater control over their choices, learning, and lives. Though students used nonviolent means of protest, the authorities intervened, and many students were wounded. Angry students wrote rebellious slogans on university walls, including "Anarchy is I."[2] Many of the slogans were inspired by Debord's actions or quotations from his writings. Later, his work influenced students of art, film, and cultural theory.

Nuclear Protests

Before Debord influenced student protestors, others around the world were protesting the rise of nuclear weapons. The late 1950s and early 1960s saw the advancement of a new threat to world peace and security in the form of these

"If a revolutionary movement is to succeed, no form of organization whatever must be allowed to dam its spontaneous flow. It must evolve its own forms and structures."[3]

—*Daniel Cohn-Bendit, active in student protests in France, 1968* weapons. The first atomic bomb, dropped by the United States on Hiroshima, Japan, in 1945, was followed shortly afterward by a second on the city of Nagasaki, Japan. The bombing marked the end of World War II and the start of the atomic age, the era of nuclear weapons.

Concerned citizens around the world responded to the rise of nuclear weapons in the form of protests. The largest organizing body of these protests was the Campaign for Nuclear Disarmament (CND), which started in London in 1958. What began as a public meeting of activists and others alarmed by the rise of nuclear weapons grew into a widespread coalition that continues to this day. The CND has been responsible for nonviolent protests against nuclear weapons around the world for more than 50 years. Efforts by members of the CND to rise up and speak out against governmental actions, specifically the buildup of nuclear weapons, are anarchist not in name but in sensibility. Activists participate voluntarily in protests that challenge and sometimes halt government actions.

Over the next two decades, protests against nuclear weapons centered on the Cold War between the United States and the Soviet Union. The two superpowers used tactical and strategic methods rather than actual combat in an effort to avoid the use of deadly nuclear weapons. Still, their methods focused on stockpiling nuclear weapons. Citizens became deeply concerned about the safety of making these deadly weapons, and activists protested the buildup of nuclear weapons and the development of new weapons facilities.

One of the primary protest groups to develop out of this time period in the United States was the Clamshell Alliance, founded in 1976 by a group of activists in New England. The group united in protesting President Richard Nixon's program to build 1,000 nuclear power plants by the year 2000. In addition to the weapons being potentially disastrous, the group was concerned about the safety of the plants. The Clamshell Alliance held nonviolent protests against institutions in an effort to halt the progress of the nuclear power plants.

The nonviolent protests of the CND, the Clamshell Alliance, and others involved in contesting nuclear weapons continues to this day. Their efforts relate to the anarchists' mission to create a safe and prosperous society for all. Their obstruction of official and governmental activities is similarly anarchist in spirit.

Vietnam Protests

During the 1960s, other war protests took place. Around the world, students led protests against the Vietnam War and governmental interference in personal lives. Anti-Vietnam War protests erupted in major international cities, including Paris, Amsterdam, Mexico City, Tokyo, and New York. While students protested the war, they also revolted against what is known as the military-industrial complex, the relationship between the military and the businesses that support it.

For the students, this signified valuing products over human life and freedom. Like Read and Debord, the protestors resented the control this structure imposed on their identities and choices.

ANARCHISM'S INFLUENCE ON CIVIL DISOBEDIENCE

During the 1950s and 1960s, Martin Luther King Jr. led US civil rights activists in protesting unjust laws and promoting equal rights for African Americans. King was committed to civil disobedience, or nonviolent protest. His ideas were influenced by the writings of Henry David Thoreau, a US writer who advocated the opposition of unjust laws and whose ideas are often associated with anarchism, and also by the nonviolent protests of Indian lawyer and activist Mohandas Gandhi, who was, in turn, influenced by Christian anarchist Leo Tolstoy. King's development of civil disobedience was inspired in part by the ideas and actions of this anarchist predecessor.

Punk Rock

Anarchism is flexible. Just as anarchist concepts re-emerged in the protests of the 1960s, they gained a new interpretation during the 1970s in punk rock. Punk musicians and fans responded to the kind of disquiet and apathy that grew out of capitalism and excessive commercialism.

Among the most famous punk bands is the Sex Pistols. The English musicians identified themselves with anarchism and spoke out against class divisions in England. The band's debut single, "Anarchy in the UK," released in 1976, became an unofficial anthem of punk

The music of the Sex Pistols represented anarchists' attitudes of the time.

rock and the anarchist thinking of that time. Punk rock gave a loud, brash, and unapologetic voice to the angst and frustration protestors and activists had expressed in prior decades. It also provided a powerful vision of antiauthoritarianism. ⌘

Anarchism and Revolution

Historically, revolution has been a primary form of social and political transformation. In each of the world's great revolutions, people have risen up from difficult conditions to seek new laws and new forms of government that would be more equitable and less oppressive and provide more freedoms. The major revolutions throughout history, from the French and American Revolutions of the late eighteenth century to the Russian Revolution in the early twentieth, were fought for such changes.

The French Revolution was fought to abolish oppressive rule in France.

The history of anarchism runs parallel to that of revolution.

In the American Revolution, culminating with the signing of the Declaration of Independence in July 1776, English settlers in North American colonies fought to establish their freedom from England. One of the primary motivations was the freedom to practice any form of religion.

Little more than a decade later, in July 1789, the French people united to storm the Bastille, a notorious prison, and to overthrow the monarchy of Louis XVI. Unfair conditions had persisted for the poor working class at the hands of wealthy royalty and landowners. The people's revolt marked the start of the French Revolution that ultimately established a more fair and equitable government.

Neither the American nor French Revolutions was anarchist in nature. In fact, both of the new governments that emerged actively fought against anarchists

"The anarchist sees revolutionary change as something immediate, something we must do now, where we are, where we live, where we work. It means starting this moment to do away with authoritarian, cruel relationships—between parents and children, between one kind of worker and another. Such revolutionary action cannot be crushed like an armed uprising. It takes place in everyday life, in the tiny crannies where the powerful but clumsy hands of state power cannot easily reach."[1]

—*Howard Zinn, historian and professor*

in the early twentieth century. What is interesting about these two revolutions in relation to anarchism is the way the people directly participated to change their social and political systems.

Still, the full enactment of revolution, for the anarchist, would do away with the state altogether. Russian-American anarchist Alexander Berkman sympathized with all rebellions against authority when he wrote,

> But blind rebellion without definite object and purpose is not revolution. . . . Revolution is rebellion become conscious of its aims. Revolution is social when it strives for fundamental change.[2]

In this way, Berkman pointed to the definition of an anarchist revolution, which would replace the institution of the state with the organization of people into voluntary associations acting on mutual consent.

Anarchist Revolution

For anarchists, changing from one government to another does not constitute the change they seek. What an anarchist revolution looks like has been debated among anarchists and others seeking change. Around the turn of the twentieth century, revolution was modeled more or less on the French Revolution: a radical, spontaneous, and violent overthrow of the government. Even today, anarchists continue to press for a full social, cultural, and ideological revolution, but most acknowledge that it would not take the form of revolution in the traditional sense. Instead, an anarchist revolution would be slower and come from within society where groups of individuals work for change.

An anarchist revolution involves shifting the hearts and minds of the men and women who will create a new society based on natural self-organization of communities, the unfolding of individual freedoms, and communal co-ownership of resources. In the creation of this kind of society, anarchist Herbert Read wrote,

> The main thing is to establish your principles— the principles of equity, of individual freedom, of workers' control. The community then aims at the establishment of these principles from the starting point of local needs and local conditions. That they must be established by revolutionary means is perhaps inevitable.[3]

Bakunin, too, believed that change must first be planted in the hearts and minds of the people before any form of revolution can take place.

Noam Chomsky, the contemporary scholar, linguist, and activist inspired by anarchism at a young age, said in a 2004 interview,

> The main strains of anarchism have been very concerned with means. They have often tended to try to follow the idea that Bakunin expressed, that you should build the seeds of the future society within the existing one, and have been very extensively involved in educational work: forming collectives, small collectives and larger ones, and other kinds of organizations.[4]

"There are periods in the life of human society when revolution becomes an imperative necessity, when it proclaims itself as inevitable. New ideas germinate everywhere, seeking to force their way into the light, to find an application in life; everywhere they are opposed by the inertia of those whose interest is to maintain the old order; they suffocate in the stifling atmosphere of prejudice and traditions."[5]

—*Peter Kropotkin, anarchist, philosopher, and activist*

This kind of organizational preparation is a necessary part of the process of a cultural, economic, and ideological revolution.

Visions of Revolution

A large-scale revolution according to anarchist ideals has not yet created the substantial and long-lasting change that anarchists seek, but revolutions throughout the world have caused changes in government. Sometimes, the new system ends up being more closed and corrupt than the old one, but overall, revolution has served to replace oppressive governments with more just ones. In this way, revolution as a force for change has gradually shifted the balance of power in many parts of the world. Anarchists share with many revolutionaries the common goal of preserving the full and autonomous freedom of each individual without oppression, exploitation, or hierarchy.

Ideas about what an anarchist revolution would look like can be roughly divided into two camps. One group of anarchists supports gradual change, participating in existing governmental systems as a necessary step toward achieving liberation from oppression. This group includes Proudhon, who served briefly in the French National Assembly, and Spanish anarchist and feminist Montseny, who also served in government. Proudhon and Montseny were equally radical in their ideas and goals for a society free of government, but they were also realists who wanted to create change within the existing political system as an initial step toward changing the entire structure.

Another route to anarchist revolution is the complete rejection of any form of participation in government. This can be found in Bakunin and the American anarchist Goldman, who definitively renounced participation in government. Bakunin believed in working directly with people to educate and inspire them to take control of their society. His support of propaganda by the deed seems to have come from his idea that power structures will not dismantle without a fight.

Planning Ahead

Those seeking a change in society can look to history and learn from the past. As such, anarchists and others study and learn from the successes and failures of past revolutionaries. What the majority of anarchist philosophers seem to have gleaned from revolutionary history is the necessity of preparation in order for a successful revolution, whether spontaneous or gradual, to sustain real and lasting change.

The societal change that anarchism describes is radical. It involves organization and ownership of resources not from the top down but from the bottom up. It seeks to create the conditions

THE HUNGARIAN REVOLUTION

After World War II, Hungary, Poland, and other Eastern European countries came under the control of the Soviet Union, led by the totalitarian Communist, Joseph Stalin. In 1956, the Hungarian people rose up against oppressive leadership. Students, workers, and other citizens joined in fighting for freedom from Soviet control. They achieved early victories over Soviet forces, and it looked like a truce was imminent between the government of Moscow and the Hungarian people, led by their president, Imre Nagy. But the Hungarian Revolution was defeated by a sudden, crushing attack by the Soviet Union. President Nagy was captured, and many Hungarians were killed. Though it ultimately failed, the Hungarian Revolution represents a people's revolution against oppressive rule.

for order, spontaneity, and the natural flow of life in the present. Anarchism rejects authority, oppression, hierarchy, and any system that allows one to exploit or subjugate another. For example, most anarchists are strictly against capitalism, the dominant economic structure in the world today, and would like to see it dissolved.

While anarchists at different times in history have defined themselves and their objectives against specific governments and cultures, the overall goals of anarchist society are distinct from anything that has ever existed for vast amounts of people in the modern world. The kind of large-scale fundamental change inherent in an anarchist revolution requires preparation, education, and planting of the seeds of possibility to succeed.

Initially, Proudhon outlined a phased approach to anarchist revolution. In his view, the eighteenth-century transition in Europe from serfdom to wage-labor—from something akin to slavery to being paid for work—was one step of a larger process. It brought more freedom to the worker but did not offer the form of unfettered freedom that remained the goal of anarchists. The ultimate evolution of this change would occur when workers controlled their own time, process, resources, and products. In a capitalist system, workers have more freedom than serfdom, but the owners of corporations own the means of production and control schedules and products. This places wealth in the hands of the few, rather than the many, and explains why the leaders of the anarchist movement throughout history have been deeply opposed to capitalism.

In one way or another, the vast majority of anarchist thinkers have historically seen anarchism as the result of an evolutionary process. While they have stressed that change begins in the present, and advocated direct action over theory, many have been realistic about the way in which it would come to pass.

The Psychology of Change

Regardless of which kind of change—gradual or sudden—contemporary activists follow, maintaining an anarchist society would require real imagination and courage. Judith Suissa, professor and author of *Anarchism and Educations*, wrote,

> *Even after a successful social revolution which dismantles the state there will still be a vital need for an education which can nurture the social virtues on which an anarchist society might be built.*[6]

One of the first anarchists to discuss the psychology of change in detail was Gustav Landauer, a German philosopher and anarchist-socialist who worked during the early twentieth century. Landauer brought to anarchism a sense that the human psyche, or consciousness, was integral to the kind of changes that anarchists sought. Landauer saw the human psyche as inexplicably linked to community, a link that was threatened by the modern, industrial world. Rather than seeing government as something to overthrow,

Landauer saw it as a form of relationship that people could change by changing their own ideas and attitudes. For Landauer, change began with each individual.

This line of thinking is perpetuated in the way that anarchism and anarchistic ideals have played themselves out in contemporary times. Chomsky has also emphasized the importance of consciousness-raising:

But, as anyone involved in any form of activism knows—say the Women's Movement—one of the first tasks is to get people to understand that they are living under conditions of oppression and domination.[7]

"The state is a condition, a certain relationship between human beings, a mode of human behavior; we destroy it by contracting other relationships, by behaving differently."[8]

—*Gustav Landauer, philosopher and anarchist-socialist*

Chomsky explained how capitalism conditions people to turn away from their innate compassion and solidarity, instincts that would inspire equitable social solutions. He cited the beginnings of this shift in the 1920s, when science introduced ways to make the modern worker more productive and less emotional. These techniques, known as scientific management, or Taylorism, after their founder, Frederick Taylor, regimented workers' behavior with the

According to Chomsky, automation, such as sorting machines, encouraged workers' emotional suppression.

goal of greater productivity. These behaviors were then applied to other aspects of society, including schools, advertising, and the organization of stores. ⌘

7

Anarchist Economics

From the first anarchist scholars and activists up to those of contemporary times, economics has played a pivotal role in their conceptions of society and change. If, anarchism contends, individuals have control over their own work and livelihood, they have the freedom to grow and develop their own strengths, interests, and capabilities. If, on the other hand, people toil under the rules and authority of others, and for the profit of others, their freedom and capacity to grow, develop, and enjoy life are greatly curtailed.

In an anarchist society, goods would not be purchased. Instead, they would be distributed equally among community members.

In a contemporary context, this is exemplified by capitalism, a system in which individuals or corporations can grow exponentially at the expense of the labor and capital, or investment, of others. Of course, individuals choose to work and invest at their own discretion. But in a capitalist system, wage-labor is often the only choice.

Capitalism and anarchism are built on conflicting values and are fundamentally opposed. Anarchism sees competition as against natural growth and freedom, which are dependent on collaboration. Capitalism, on the other hand, thrives on competition. From its inception, anarchism has been in opposition to capitalism's negative effects, including the exploitation of wage-labor and capital, the control exercised by a boss over workers, and wealth or class differentiations.

Initially, many workers saw the system of wage-labor as a means to subjugate and exploit the working class. Because workers needed money to survive, they had to accept whatever job and conditions were offered. A capitalist economy took away workers' choices and decreased their standard of living. Given the relationship of work to such things as quality of life, the ability to exercise personal freedoms, and equality among people, it is no surprise that virtually every formulation of anarchistic society has integrated economic with cultural and ideological change.

Value and Price

To a person accustomed to living in a capitalist system, where money purchases goods, and capital in the hands of the few is intended to fuel economic growth, anarchist economics might sound murky and strange. In *The ABC of Anarchism*, Alexander Berkman answered questions posed to him by an imaginary interviewer. His explanation of anarchist economics gets at the heart of how very different anarchist conceptions of labor, value, and price are from capitalist views. Value, Berkman wrote, cannot be determined, because "the same thing may be worth a lot to one person while it is worth nothing or very little to another."[1] Value, to the anarchist, is not measured by money but by quality of life. Price, on the other hand, is determined by the market and the laws of supply and demand. But, Berkman continued,

> The exchange of commodities by means of prices leads to profit-making, to taking advantage and exploitation; in short, to some form of capitalism. If you do away with profits, you cannot have any price system, nor any system of wages or payment. That means that exchange must be according to value.[2]

Berkman explained that in an anarchist society, products and labor would be exchanged and distributed according to necessity and shared equally by everyone. In accordance with anarchist principles, no person is more valuable than another, and each would receive what he or she needed to live freely and happily. This includes the opportunity to develop interests and skills to do the work that each person chooses to do. No form of work would be considered more important or more valuable than another or merit extra resources. If one person wanted to be a doctor, he or she would study and practice medicine. Another might want to teach children, and another, build houses.

In an anarchist society, as Berkman and others have described it, there would be no discrimination. All would participate in the making of an equitable society, including caring for the sick, the elderly, and the disabled. At the same time, because everyone would participate in the necessary work, there would be ample time for friends and family, leisure, and exploring the arts, spiritual pursuits, or new interests and talents.

EQUITY STORE

In 1827, American anarchist Josiah Warren opened a store in Cincinnati, Ohio. Warren believed that authority caused corruption. He believed in complete individual liberty. His store was an equity store, based on trade instead of money. People worked in the store, exchanging time and labor for food.

Mutualism

Proudhon's ideas about anarchism developed simultaneously with his system of economics, known as mutualism. This is based on the belief that workers or artisans should maintain ownership of their products and means of production, such as land and tools. Cooperatively, workers would control the making of watches, jeans, or other products that could then be freely traded with other workers' collectives so each group could procure needed resources, food, and other goods.

Proudhon was deeply opposed to capital, which he saw as a form of exploitation of one person over another. Similarly, he opposed the practice of lending money at interest and recommended mutual aid societies, or credit unions, where people could obtain loans at no cost. Ever realistic and idealistic, Proudhon looked ahead to a time when organization and ownership would gradually shift out of the hands of government and business and into the hands of the people. His system of free credit would allow people to acquire needed money or capital without being subjected to exploitation and subjugation. In the meantime, though, he knew that money and capital would remain a necessity.

Anarcho-syndicalism

One of the important legacies of twentieth century anarchism is the economic system known as anarcho-syndicalism. Developed in the early twentieth century, anarcho-syndicalism has roots in craftspeople's guilds from medieval times, Swiss watchmakers' guilds of the seventeenth and eighteenth centuries, and the Paris Commune of 1871. In each of these instances, workers and craftspeople maintained ownership of their resources, work, and products.

Anarcho-syndicalism is based on the formation of independent syndicates—similar to trade unions, collectives, or federations of workers. These syndicates then freely trade goods and services with others in a system of mutual collaboration.

Derived from the French word *Syndicalisme*, syndicalism is a worker-controlled economic system. Anarchists and Communists alike have seen it as a means for social revolution. The differences between anarcho-syndicalism and early communism are slim. Communism, however, retained some form of centralized authority, while anarchism relied solely on independent collaboration among autonomous syndicates. Another difference is that communism focused on political revolution, while anarcho-syndicalism focused on social revolution.

In practice, communism began to take root in Russia but was taken over and perverted into a system of totalitarian socialism in the Soviet Union. Anarcho-syndicalism was briefly

SWISS WATCHMAKERS

During the sixteenth century, a watch industry developed in Geneva, Switzerland. Before long, the watches were known for quality and craftsmanship. In 1601, Swiss workers established the Watchmakers' Guild of Geneva. Approximately 100 years later, the city had many watchmakers. Many moved to the Jura Mountains, where they continued to thrive as independent craftsmen, selling their popular watches around the world. The watchmakers of the Swiss Jura were inspirational to later anarchists and anarcho-syndicalist theorists.

successful in Spain in the years prior to the Spanish Revolution.

Marxism and anarchism shared the idea of worker control, and both were part of the formation of the First International. Marxism spread more rapidly, and anarchists went another direction from the main body of the workers' federation, but both anarchism and Marxism had a powerful impact on workers' rights and the labor movement around the world, including the development of trade unions.

> "We would thank anyone to point out to us what function, if any, the state can have in an economic organization, where private property has been abolished and in which parasitism and special privilege have no place."[3]
>
> —*Diego Abad de Santillan, anarcho-syndicalist economist*

The Labor Movement

How workers are treated in their day-to-day lives on the job is directly related to the economic system under which they toil. For example, in a capitalist system, where a small group controls the means of production and receives the majority of the profit, workers must abide by the rules and the regulations of the few who own everything. Workers do not own their own products or control their daily working conditions.

In the early twentieth century, when capitalism was becoming the predominant economic system, workers labored under far harsher conditions than they do today. Conditions have markedly improved for workers in the United States, Europe, Latin America and some, though not all, other parts of the world in the past century. In large part, this is due to the protests and activism of the labor movement during the 1930s.

Though a minority in the labor movement in the United States, anarchists played an important role.

Unions, also called trade unions or labor unions, are organizations of workers who share common goals and work for fair conditions. Unions are very similar to syndicates; however, syndicates in their ideal form are more deeply embedded in the society and culture because their members co-own the resources and control their own work and products. In the early twentieth century, union membership grew significantly in many parts of the world. Anarchists signed

COMMUNAL LIVING IN JUDAISM

Kibbutz is a Hebrew word for communal living settlement. In Israel, groups of people have voluntarily lived communally in kibbutzim for many years. Jewish pioneers from Eastern Europe founded the first kibbutz, dedicated to creating a new and more holistic way of life, long before Israel became a state in 1948. Today, these communities remain an important part of Israeli culture and economy. Kibbutzim are based on principles of equality, mutual aid, cooperation, social justice, and joint ownership of property. Kibbutzim are not anarchist but share the same principles as anarchist communities.

Labor strikes, such as the ladies tailors' strike of 1910, are used to initiate change beneficial to workers.

up millions of workers in unions in Spain and parts of Europe.

A workers' strike occurs when groups of workers leave their job for a period of time. Workers have used strikes to protest unfair conditions and instigate positive change. For example, in the early part of the twentieth century, millions of US workers protested for the eight-hour workday.

Though marked improvements have been made in workers' conditions since this time, the treatment of workers—including fair labor laws, adequate wages, safe conditions, and opportunities to grow and develop—remains a large concern for both workers and activists worldwide. From an anarchist point of view, these problems will persist as long as capitalism keeps people tied to wage-labor and the marketplace. ⌘

Anarchism and Art

Anarchism requires people to see, and then to drop, their habitual dependence on authority. Among the possible structures a society could take, anarchism may require the biggest leap of faith and the greatest stretch of the imagination. It is no wonder it has attracted so many artists, poets, and writers whose work depends on creativity and imagination.

Seeing Possibility

Art and anarchism attract the same sort of creative and independent people who often see

Some artists are drawn to anarchism because it encourages imagination and possibility.

the importance of possibility. The translation of *anarchy* ("without ruler") has a variety of potential interpretations. It could take the form of the conventional meaning of anarchy, chaos and disorder, but it certainly need not. If several people find themselves in a room together, waiting for a stuck elevator to be fixed, they may not have rules of behavior to follow, but it is likely that they would accommodate one another, help each other as needed, and generally get along peaceably.

Anarchism, as a set of ideas and a way of life, asks people to imagine a way of life completely different from the one they know. It allows people space to develop and grow naturally, pursue their interests, participate in a community, share resources, and determine their own destiny. For much of history, this has not been the case. But anarchists hold that it is not only possible, it is necessary. Like artists, anarchists imagine something that is possible but has not yet been created. In order for creation to happen, anarchists maintain an intense loyalty to the belief that people are inherently capable, creative, and compassionate. Anarchists of all stripes are consistent in the idea that, given the right conditions, peace and order will thrive alongside mutual cooperation.

Supporting Beauty and Individuality

Anarchism is unique among social structures in its embrace of independence, natural development and growth, and the acceptance of dreams, creativity, and enjoyment as integral to life. In this sense, it fits as a complement to art. No other social or political structure so openly allows and encourages the kind of mentality necessary for art—namely, the time and freedom to imagine, create, grow, and develop something that has not existed before. About prevalent social order and politics, historian Howard Zinn wrote,

> The order of politics, as we have known it in the world, is an order imposed on society, neither desired by most people, nor directed to their needs. It is therefore chaotic and destructive. Politics grates on our sensibilities. It violates the elementary requirement of aesthetics—it is devoid of beauty.[1]

Anarchism and art both address the unfolding of individuality. Psychologist Sigmund Freud first identified what he saw as human dependence on the authority of the father in the formation of the personality. This habit of authority is then transferred to a social setting, government. Art critic, poet, and anarchist Herbert Read indicated that anarchism supports individuation, or the development of the unique individual, beyond the authority of the father or the state. Read outlined the inherent problem that art faced in organizational structures: "Capitalism does not challenge poetry in principle—it merely treats it with ignorance, indifference, and unconscious cruelty."[2] In totalitarian systems, art fares no better. He continued, "Both fascism and Marxism are fully aware of the power of the poet, and because the poet is powerful, they wish to use him for their own political purposes."[3]

Art in the Heyday

Anarchist interest in the arts extended to writing, theater, and other pursuits during anarchism's heyday. Anarchists enjoyed a lively cultural life at the turn of the century. Historian Richard Sonn wrote, "Anarchists expressed their solidarity at a grass-roots level, in the cafés and union halls, in anarchist libraries and schools, and through the anarchist press."[4] Their numerous periodicals were similarly expressive, using slang and street language, art, poetry, testimonials, and manifestos to spread their message of unfettered freedom.

Anarchism attracted artists, poets, bohemians, and dreamers. In part, they were drawn to the message of independence and possibility. Marxism, vying with anarchism for public attention, appealed to industrial workers rather than artisans and craftspeople. Marxist newspapers tended to want artists to create images and texts that the public would readily understand. But a new form of art, modernism, had captured the imaginations of painters and poets alike, and they wanted to express their ideas as they chose. Anarchist papers were more sympathetic to these artists' interests.

Many now-famous artists and poets were drawn to anarchism. Some, such as Camille Pisarro and Maximilien Luce, contributed to anarchist papers and participated in the movement.

Others, Impressionist and Cubist painters among them, were sympathetic to anarchism, including Pablo Picasso, Maurice Vlaminck, and André Derain. Poets were attracted to anarchism for similar reasons, the freedom to express ideas in new and challenging ways, even if the public would not readily understand them. Writers, including poet Stéphane Mallarmé and critic Félix Fénéon, contributed to anarchist publications. In 1968, an important abstract painter, Barnett Newman, wrote a thoughtful forward to Peter Kropotkin's writings collected in *Memoirs of a Revolutionist.*

> "The poet or the painter or the composer, if he is more than an entertainer, is a man who moves us with some joyful or tragic interpretation of the meaning of life; who foretells our human destiny or who celebrates the beauty and significance of our natural environment; who creates in us the wonder and the terror of the unknown."[5]
>
> —Herbert Read, anarchist, philosopher, and poet

An Art of the Absurd

Just as World War I was starting, and anarchism, for the most part, quieted or was crushed, a new artistic movement called Dada commenced. Dada artists and poets rejected the depersonalization and regimentation of culture and work they saw in society's march toward progress in the form of rationality, industrialization, and capitalism. They protested the war and aspects of modern society that led to war. They challenged rigid ideas of taste, beauty, and order. Dadaists created an art of the absurd, challenging accepted societal beliefs and ideas. Their art reflected what they experienced as the absurdity of the times. Most Dadaists were not anarchist by name, but their protest against authority and dogma in favor of creativity and humanity, are anarchistic in nature.

Dadaists were among the first to use collage; they took words and images out of context and pasted them together in new ways. They did not intend to make meaning, but rather anti-meaning, to protest the excessive rationality around them and the contrasting cacophony of war. Among Dadaists were painter and poet Hans Arp; collage artist Kurt Schwitters, who turned his home into a large, dynamic collage; and photographer Man Ray, who made photographs without a camera. Dada poets included Italian poet Filippo Tommaso Emilio Marinetti, a founder of the Futurists, a group of artists rejecting tradition, and Tristan Tzara, poet and author of the *Dada Manifesto*.

Predating contemporary art and a contemporary activist stance, the deeply influential artist Marcel Duchamp chose not to identify with any movement. Duchamp's ready-made sculptures of objects such as toilets

> "I am against systems, the most acceptable system is on principle to have none. To complete oneself, to perfect oneself in one's own littleness, to fill the vessel with one's individuality, to have the courage to fight for and against thought, the mystery of bread, the sudden burst of an infernal propeller into economic lilies."[6]
>
> —*Tristan Tzara, Dada poet*

and bicycle wheels shocked the art world and drastically changed ideas about and definitions of art.

As anarchism dissipated, in both name and deed, its ideas continued to evolve in Dadaists—and in artists who followed in their footsteps. Art movements and forms including surrealism, arte povera, fluxus, punk rock, performance art, and tagging have their roots in anarchist thinking. They challenge the status quo and subvert accepted ideas about taste, beauty, society, and ways of thinking and behaving. Contemporary intellectuals and activists in the anarchist tradition tend not to identify with the theory by name but associate themselves with its principles and ideas.

Anarchism and Writing

The relationship between anarchism and writing is lengthy and diverse. From its beginning, anarchism was articulated and spread through writing. Although direct action over theory has been integral to anarchism, the relationship between action and writing is particularly prominent in a vision of society that has yet to take place on a large scale for an extended period of time. Creating a picture of the society they envisioned, and the government they rejected, was vital to anarchists. Without it, it would be difficult for anyone else to imagine what anarchists wanted and to support their cause.

Anarchism supports an integrated culture where art and science, math and literature, farming and building, are valued equally. Because of this holistic vision, distinctions among theorists, poets, journalists, novelists, and other kinds of writers are not as finite in relation to anarchism as in other fields. Two of anarchism's primary writers of the twentieth century were also poets and literary figures: Englishman Herbert Read in the 1950s and Canadian George Woodcock in the 1960s.

Newspapers, magazines, and periodicals have always been important parts of the anarchist movement. They were relatively easy and cheap to produce and spread the message quickly while remaining dynamic, flexible, and relevant to working people, activists, artists, and other readers. Anarchist papers have included the early *Le Révolté* in Switzerland and then in France and *Tucker's Liberty* in the United States. From 1906 to 1917, Goldman published and edited the publication *Mother Earth*, which had 8,000 subscribers at its height.

Other writers and poets wrote honestly about anarchist ideas in their work. These included the

FEMALE ANARCHIST AND WRITER

In 1886, English anarchist Charlotte Wilson and Kropotkin cofounded *Freedom*, the oldest and longest-running anarchist newspaper. Wilson served as the editor and publisher for eight years. An active lecturer, writer, and publisher, Wilson also served as the inspiration for characters in political novels, including *A Girl Among the Anarchists*, written by Isabel Meredith and published in 1903.

award-winning fiction of Leo Tolstoy, the renowned plays of Henrik Ibsen, and the influential fiction and essays of George Orwell, Aldous Huxley, Albert Camus, and Edward Abbey. In the vein of Orwell and Huxley, whose fiction created fearful visions of a totalitarian future, contemporary science-fiction books and films further dramatize anarchistic fears of an overly controlled, intensely hierarchical, and negatively technological future. Interestingly, a shift occurred between the nineteenth and twentieth centuries, with the earlier writers articulating anarchism's possibilities and later writers exaggerating its most potent predictions for the future of society. ⌘

9

Forms of Anarchism

Although anarchists share a basic belief in the compassion, creativity, and capacity of human nature, and believe the state should be abolished, they differ in thinking about how to self-organize and how to achieve change. Noam Chomsky, influenced by anarchism from a young age, said,

> There have been many styles of thought and action that have been referred to as "anarchist." It would be hopeless to try to encompass all of these conflicting tendencies in some general theory or ideology.[1]

Noam Chomsky has been influenced by anarchism, but he chooses not to be defined as an anarchist.

In recent history, many thinkers and activists with anarchistic leanings do not adhere to the name *anarchist* or often to any label or -ism. Many of these, Chomsky among them, are deeply aware of, and influenced by, anarchism but have opted not to use the name *anarchist* because of its negative associations.

Many anarchists refute the division into categories, but because these help to make sense of information and knowledge, historians and some anarchists have divided anarchism into loose groupings according to values or methodology. Although anarchist remains a sensibility, a way of thinking about society and a way of life, more than a name by which to identify someone, a brief description of some of the main schools is helpful in understanding the possibilities contained within anarchism.

Mutualism

One of the key founders of anarchism, Proudhon, expressed the economic idea of mutualism. In this form of anarchism, the means of production remain in individual workers' hands, and they freely choose to form mutual associations in order to be more productive or profitable. This economic idea has come to be understood as one school of thought in anarchism.

For Proudhon, capitalism was rife with exploitation and subjugation. In opposition to this, mutualism gave workers control over industry and craft. Rather than a minority profiting from the majority, as is the case in capitalism, the majority would own their own work and efforts. Workers operating in the system of mutualism would have opportunities to expand their production and profits through voluntary collaboration. For example, if one made watches, and another specialized in gold chains, they could opt to work together to sell watches that had gold chains.

Collectivist Anarchism

Collectivist anarchism, also called anarcho-collectivism, arose after mutualism. Bakunin was its primary proponent. In collectivist anarchism, the means of production are collectivized, meaning that they are co-owned by an association of workers. This is different from mutualism, in which individual workers or voluntary groups own their tools and products.

Similar to other forms of anarchism, workers in an anarcho-collectivist system participate voluntarily. But once members of a collective, they each have a stake in the whole, including the means of production and the products generated by the collective.

Workers' collectives freely associate or collaborate with other collectives. To distribute profits in anarcho-collectivism, the group would determine the amount of work an individual had done and pay him or her accordingly.

Communist Anarchism

Both anarchism and communism began forming in Europe in the early nineteenth century.

They shared many similarities and, for a time, competed among working people for popularity. In the nineteenth century, anarchism was more popular than communism. After World War I, communism prevailed over anarchism.

Both anarchism and communism proposed radical ways of thinking about society. Because of this, they have often been confused as being the same thing by those uninvolved in either. Adolf Fischer, one of the anarchists tried and killed in Chicago during the Haymarket trial, has been quoted by more than one anarchist historian for his statement: "Every anarchist is a socialist, but not every socialist is necessarily an anarchist."[2] Just as radical feminists and extremist punk rockers occupied the furthest left position of the 1970s culture, anarchists have always embodied the most radical form of socialism.

ANARCHA-FEMINISM

Anarchist feminism, also called anarcha-feminism, is a school of anarchist thought that blends aspects of feminism and anarchism. It strives to eliminate hierarchies, specifically male-dominated hierarchies. Unlike other forms of anarchism that describe a position or stance within the whole, anarcha-feminists distinguish themselves from anarchism, which they primarily see as stuck in a male-dominated structure. Like anarchists, anarcha-feminists self-organize into loosely connected groups in different countries to communicate and disseminate information about gender issues, women's health, women in history, or, as many of them prefer, herstory, and social and political issues.

Communist anarchism, as defined by Kropotkin, opposes centralization. It includes the idea of shared resources and collective ownership but relies on anarchist principles of individuality, autonomy, and diversity. In addition to workers co-owning their tools and products, Communist anarchists distribute not according to the amount of work done, but according to people's needs. For example, if a man in the collective were to fall ill and be unable to work, he would still receive whatever share of the profits were needed, even if his illness necessitated that he be given bigger profits than others received. According to Kropotkin, the vast majority of anarchist workers fall into the category of Communist anarchists.

Syndicalism

The next school of thought that developed within anarchism was syndicalism, the economic system also referred to as anarcho-syndicalism. This arose in the late nineteenth and early twentieth centuries and was the predominant form of anarchism practiced in Spain prior to the Spanish Civil War. Syndicalism, as a way of organizing labor and society, is an important legacy from anarchism's heyday.

In a syndicalist system, workers organize themselves into groups referred to as syndicates. These syndicates own their own means of production and products. Like trade unions, syndicates band together for the workers' common good. But syndicalism is more than just an economic system. It is also a means of organizing society into voluntary communities. These communities have control over their resources and products and decide how to share and distribute them. Syndicates can then trade or collaborate with other groups.

Syndicalism is a way of achieving lasting change through a reorganization of society that begins with the workers and extends to families and communities. As compared to communism, which promotes political change, syndicalism is a social and economic system that promotes social change.

> "What compels me to fight this society is, of course, outrage over injustice, a love of freedom, and a feeling of responsibility for perpetuating and enlarging the human spirit—its beauty, creativity, and latent capacity to improve the world. I do not care to come to terms with an irrational society that corrodes all that is valuable in humanity, that eats away at all that is beautiful and noble in the human experience."[3]
>
> —Murray Bookchin, anarchist and social ecologist

Individualist Anarchism

While the majority of anarchists have practiced Communist anarchism or some form of socialism based on shared resources, there is a branch of anarchist thought that diverges from community-centered ideas and practices.

What has come to be known as individualist anarchism began with the work of German philosopher Max Stirner, who wrote just before

Marx and Bakunin. Stirner's sense was that the individual supersedes all else. Completely disregarding society or community, Stirner's thinking was egoistic.

Stirner's theory is refuted by an assortment of thinkers. Some people think Marx developed his social theories in part to refute Stirner. For Bakunin and other Communist anarchists, Stirner represented a dangerous denial of human's interconnection to society. German anarchist Gustav Landauer also argued against Stirner, proposing that there is no individual without community because the former grows from the latter. But Stirner's ideas found resonance with his more famous peer in German philosophy, Friedrich Nietzsche. In particular, Nietzsche's idea of the Super-man—the singular, noble individual who alone can overcome the burdens of society—echoes Stirner. At the turn of the century, Stirner and Nietzsche were embraced by a small group of artists and intellectuals.

Proudhon, the father of anarchism, is sometimes described as an individualist anarchist due to his support of workers' ownership of their own products, but this characterization is misleading. Unlike individualist anarchists, Proudhon valued freedom in the context of community. His work and writings are wholly dedicated to a functioning society and emphasize the way artisans and laborers can be empowered with collective organization to gradually replace the functions of government.

Pacifist Anarchism

Because history and the popular media tend to emphasize anarchist violence, the type of anarchism that denies violence as a means to achieve its ends receives little attention. From the first anarchist, Proudhon, anarchists have advocated for peaceful solutions for change. This kind of anarchism has come to be known as pacifist anarchism, but when Proudhon was writing, it was simply anarchism as he understood it.

Pacifist anarchism supports the same kind of nonhierarchical society with equal rights and resources for all, but unlike many anarchists during the heyday, pacifist anarchists did not support violence as a means of achieving a free society. Instead, they advocated for peaceful and gradual changes in mind and habit. Gustav Landauer was an influential pacifist anarchist; Kropotkin, though initially supporting the doctrine of propaganda by the deed, later regretted condoning violent acts.

Many scholars also cite Leo Tolstoy as a primary example of a pacifist anarchist due to his radical interpretation of Christianity. He is also sometimes called a Christian anarchist, and, in relation, pacifist anarchism is sometimes called Christian anarchism. A philosopher and the author of *War and Peace* and *Anna Karenina*, Tolstoy was born into a noble Russian family in 1828. Later in life, he rejected wealth and privilege, embracing an ascetic lifestyle and radical Christianity. He refrained from meat, tobacco, and alcohol and dressed in the simple clothing worn by servants. In numerous essays and articles,

Leo Tolstoy's beliefs and lifestyle align with pacifist anarchist principles.

Tolstoy advised following directly in the footsteps of Jesus to practice compassion and obey one's conscience over laws or any form of government.

Environmental Anarchism

Anarchism's conception of a free, egalitarian, and holistic life includes living in harmony with the earth and sharing its resources. This puts anarchism in sympathy with the various incarnations of the environmental movements.

Murray Bookchin is the primary philosopher to create a link between anarchism and ecology. Born in New York in 1921, Bookchin was involved as an organizer in the labor movement and in the Spanish Revolution during the 1930s and 1940s.

The writings of both Marx and Kropotkin were highly influential to him. From the 1970s until his death in 2006, he developed a highly unique and influential type of contemporary anarchism, fusing anarchist principles of nondiscrimination, diversity, and holistic and harmonious living with ecology.

Bookchin brought ecology and anarchism together under the name social ecology, a body of thought he developed through books, essays, teaching, and the establishment of the Institute for Social Ecology. As defined by the institute, social ecology means, "1: a coherent radical critique of current social, political, and anti-ecological trends. 2: a reconstructive, ecological, communitarian, and ethical approach to society."[4]

Social ecology promotes a radical change in humans' relationships with one another and with the earth, stressing ways of living harmoniously with the earth and with each other that will result in natural order and naturally developing spirituality. In the small, local communities and holistic lifestyle that anarchists promoted, Bookchin saw less harmful and more

GANDHI AND TOLSTOY

Mohandas Gandhi, the Indian activist and political leader, read Tolstoy's essay "The Kingdom of God Is Within You" as a young man. Gandhi admired what Tolstoy wrote about passive resistance and nonviolence. He wrote Tolstoy a letter, and the two began a correspondence and friendship. In 1908, Tolstoy wrote *A Letter to a Hindu.*

equitable solutions to the environmental crisis than the ones being promoted at the time, such as recycling or stopping deforestation. These solutions addressed only one issue at a time, while Bookchin sought to address the larger issue of how humans relate to the world. But Bookchin distinguished social ecology from both environmentalism and New Age spiritualism, which he saw as superficial and misleading. He opposed capitalism and any suggestion that green products or technology could provide solutions to the climate crisis. ⌘

EARTH FIRST!

Not affiliated with Bookchin's radical rationality, the activist group Earth First! represents a different approach to environmental anarchism. An extreme environmental group, Earth First! was cofounded in 1979 by Dave Foreman and Mike Roselle, who were inspired by the American novelist and anarchist Edward Abbey. Initially dedicated to preserving the land of the American West, it has inspired loosely affiliated groups around the world. At times, Earth First!'s direct action tactics to stop logging, drilling, mining, and other industry harmful to the environment have put workers in harm's way.

10

Case Studies

In 1919, Nestor Makhno, a peasant turned anarchist revolutionary, put up a short-lived, but valiant, struggle against authoritarian socialism in Ukraine. He successfully led his army against highly trained military forces, and anarchists controlled Ukraine for a brief time.

Makhno was born into a poor family in Ukraine. He began working in the fields to support his family at a young age and later was trained as a printer and an ironworker. As a young man, he was exposed to anarchist ideas. The possibility of more worker control was attractive, and he joined the cause. Makhno was imprisoned from 1908 to 1917 for suspected

Leon Trotsky was once allied with the Makhnovites during their rebellion, but he ultimately killed some of their leaders.

terrorist activity and, after his release from jail, was elected chairman of the local Soviet of Workers' and Peasants' Deputies. In that role, he led the community in establishing agricultural collaboratives and local organization. Makhno also spent some time in Moscow, where he met Kropotkin.

In the face of significant military threats, Makhno organized fellow anarchists, farmers, artisans, and workers in an effort to maintain control of their villages, land, and labor. The Makhnovites, as they came to be known, led one of the most striking campaigns against authority in the history of anarchism. For a short time, they fought back the formidable forces of the Soviet armies.

Fighting under the black flag of anarchism, the Makhnovites fought in a completely voluntary manner and similarly declared the peasants they defended free from all authority. In one of his first acts in an anarchist Ukraine, Makhno, the former

ANARCHISM IN CHINA

In 1911, a Chinese-language version of the anarchist paper *New Times* was published in Paris. It included Chinese translations of anarchist writings, such as those of Peter Kropotkin. Anarchism was not widespread in China, but the first anarchist group to be established there, Shih Fu, also published a newspaper, the *People's Voice.* After the death of their leader, anarchists published his book and papers in Chinese and Esperanto, an international language popular with cultural reformers in the early twentieth century.

captive, threw open the jail doors and freed the prisoners.

For a time, the Makhnovites aided Leon Trotsky in a counter-revolution against Lenin. But Trotsky turned on the anarchists, killing the leaders. Makhno managed to escape with some of his supporters. He went to Romania, France, and finally the United States.

"It is up to the workers and peasants to organize themselves and reach mutual understanding in all areas of their lives in whatever manner they think right."[2]

—*Nestor Makhno, Ukrainian anarchist revolutionary leader*

The Rise of Anarchism in Spain

Most scholars and historians of anarchism cite Spain as the place where anarchism had the most successful and longest run as a means of organizing society. Of Spanish anarchism, historian Richard Sonn wrote,

> Spain offers the best opportunity to observe anarchism not simply as an ideal or as a motivator of violent deeds, but actually to see it in practice. It raises the possibility of an answer to the question of whether anarchism can work; whether anarchists can build as well as dream and destroy.[1]

In some ways, Spain is a country that is predisposed to the diversity and self-determination of anarchism. Its large area includes regions with unique cultural characteristics, such as Andalusia in the south and the Basque country in the north. Unlike other European countries, the Spanish government was less successful in establishing centralized rule. As early as the 1860s, vast numbers of farmers and peasants throughout Spain—including artisans, agricultural laborers, and industrial workers—joined syndicates.

During the same period, Spain was undergoing a series of political and social transformations. In 1868, after Queen Isabella was exiled, Guiseppe Fanelli, an anarchist and associate of Bakunin, went to Spain to speak about anarcho-syndicalism. Self-management took root and, before long, developed and was carried out by Spanish workers and artisans.

As the country proceeded through political upheavals and changes in leadership, membership in the Spanish International Working Men's

ITALIAN ANARCHISTS

Anarchists in Italy, as in other countries, were deeply involved in the struggle for workers' rights. In 1920, after a series of strikes and protests, members of the Italian Federation of Metal Workers were locked out of the metal factories. The workers decided to occupy the factories and continue production on their own. Workers organized a series of committees to manage technical and administrative tasks and shared all materials equitably. For a brief time, until one branch of the union came to an agreement with the factory owners, workers successfully self-managed factory production. They ended the occupation under the promise of more worker-control, which then was not granted.

Association swelled. At the same time, Modern Schools opened and spread, teaching equality and an integrated approach to education to many Spaniards.

The 1880s and 1890s witnessed the continued growth of union membership and increased violence, against both striking workers and anarchists, and in anarchist reprisals.

In 1910, in part as a result of state violence against anarchists, Spanish workers formed the union Confederación Nacional de Trabajo (CNT). At its height, CNT had more than 3 million members. Over the next two decades, through strikes and protests, workers gained some victories. But many were also imprisoned or killed as the government resisted laborers' calls for independence.

In 1933, a group of anarchists mounted a protest in the small Andalusian village of Casavieja. Declaring the town free of government and property, they laid siege to the offices of local authorities. In response, the army moved in to shut down the protest. Most of the peasant insurrectionists fled or were killed. Two brothers, along with their father, a 73-year-old anarchist hero named Seisdedos, or Six Fingers, remained and fought off the army until the military bombed their house and all three were killed.

The battle of Casavieja came at the height of the CNT struggle for power among the workers. Many anarchists had been killed or deported by the government. As a result, anarchists had organized protests in Barcelona and Valencia. The laborers in Casavieja had organized in coordination with a large labor strike. But before it happened, the CNT came to an agreement with the government, and most workers decided not to strike. News of a truce had not reached Casavieja in time for the villagers to change their plans. The tragic end in Casavieja was emblematic of a lack of communication and misinformation among the anarchist organizers. It aggravated tensions between the government and the CNT and inspired more strikes and protests.

Spanish Civil War

Between 1936 and 1939, Spanish army general Francisco Franco sought a military takeover of the country. Anarchists and other revolutionaries joined the government in resistance, raising a powerful army and fighting back Franco's forces in three major cities, Madrid, Barcelona, and Valencia. The anarchist Buenaventura Durruti emerged as an important military leader. In anarchist spirit, Durruti also encouraged the Spanish villagers to collaborate and share resources through the shortages of war.

Anarchists struggled with how much to participate with the government in fighting Franco. But when the moderate government was replaced with a more authoritarian socialist one, some Spanish anarchists, including the feminist Federica Montseny, took positions in government to support the people's cause. After a valiant fight and mutual collaboration between anarchists and the national government, Franco's forces defeated the Spanish anarchists and other revolutionaries in 1939, and Spain came under fascist rule.

The Spanish Legacy

Before its collapse, Spanish anarchism enjoyed widespread participation and numerous cultural and economic successes. During the 1880s and 1890s, anarchist schools opened across the country, teaching integral education. Also, numerous anarchist presses and cultural centers contributed to a vivid society. During the 1930s, the revolution was cultural and social. Spanish villagers occupied large areas of previously private land, living in communes with local councils. Many large factories were reorganized into collectives. Anarchist women fought for equal rights in the coalition Mujeres Libres, and a public university opened in Barcelona. Of anarchism in Spain prior to fascist rule, Chomsky said,

"I never lost touch with the anarchists and have always felt that theirs was the world I was brought up in. I don't care what you call it, but all the things that the anarchists said sixty or seventy years ago have taken on respectability. If anarchism did nothing else but serve that purpose, it was worth it. But unfortunately it has been so distorted, so misunderstood. Otherwise it might have been a great force for educating people, for liberating them."[3]

—Jeanne Levey, anarchist and founder of Parkinson's Disease Hospital, Miami, Florida

Anarchist revolution was simply destroyed by force, but during the period in which it was alive I think it was a highly successful and . . . in many ways a very inspiring testimony to the ability of poor working people to organize and manage their own affairs, extremely successfully, without coercion and control.[4]

Anarchism in Latin America

Anarchist ideas spread in Latin America—particularly in Argentina, Brazil, Colombia, Mexico, and Chile—from the early 1900s through the 1930s in most countries and in the 1960s in Chile. The history of anarchism in Latin America is not as well documented as the history of anarchism in Europe and the United States. But scholars who have addressed it agree that anarchism played an important role in workers joining trade and labor unions and in progressive cultural developments across the region.

Just as anarchism and Marxism overlapped in Europe, the history of anarchism in Latin America is intertwined with, and often very similar to, Marxist communism and socialism. To the extent that each of these theories and practices share the belief in shared ownership of property, worker-controlled production, and a lack of hierarchy, they were equally important to Latin American revolutionaries. As a result, the terms *anarchism, communism,* and *socialism* were used somewhat interchangeably in Latin America. Even though the anarchist organizing principles of mutualism and autonomy tended to prevail

During the Spanish Civil War, General Francisco Franco, center, led the fight against Spanish anarchists.

over the regimented and industrial-centered Marxism, many Latin American leftists referred to themselves as Communists.

In Latin America, women were deeply involved in the anarchist movement, perhaps more so than elsewhere. Female anarchists pushed for social change, including equal rights for women in the workplace and an abolishment of patriarchal relations between men and women. What is believed to be the first anarcha-feminist periodical, *La Voz de La Mujer*, was published in Buenos Aires, Argentina, from 1898 to 1899.

In a history of anarchism in Latin America, author Alfredo Gómez explained numerous anarchist interactions with the labor movement. These included workers' strikes in Brazil from 1917 to 1920, the influential anarchist workers' coalition, *Federación Obrera Regional*, in Argentina, and anarchist activity in Mexico, including *Casa del Obrero Mundial,* or House of the World Worker, an organizing center in Mexico City.

In addition to labor organization, anarchists pushed for progressive cultural and social reforms. Anarchists participated in reforming universities in Chile and Argentina. Numerous writers and artists contributed to building the counterculture that anarchists supported. For example, Chilean anarchist and painter Benito Rebolledo helped to form the Colonia Tolsoyana, a group of young intellectuals who wanted to practice the social equality exemplified by the Christian

MUJERES LIBRES

The Mujeres Libres, or Free Women, of Spain, is a group founded in Spain in 1936. Mujeres Libres were anarchist women that sought independence and equal rights. They started a women's college, opened maternity hospitals, expanded training for women in the workforce, and underwent military training. Some contemporary women's groups were inspired by the Mujeres Libres' short, but successful, experiences during the 1930s and are named after the Mujeres Libres.

anarchism of Tolstoy. Rebolledo included workers and the poor in his art, challenging traditional cultural hierarchies. ⌘

ANARCHIST HEALTH CARE IN CHILE

Throughout the 1930s, Chilean doctor and activist Juan Gandulfo aimed to bring a form of socialized health care to his country. Dedicated to equality for all, Gandulfo was particularly committed to elevating the quality and availability of health care for working-class and poor people. His work shows a holistic approach to anarchist society.

11

An Anarchist Legacy

With the end of the Spanish Civil War, the longest-running anarchist movement was extinguished. The name and legacy of anarchism were mostly left—except for a small group of intellectuals and activists—to society's imagination, in which anarchists morphed into bomb throwers. Although some anarchists' violent actions contributed to this image, anarchism has needed to differentiate itself from the havoc the word *anarchy* often conjures.

In light of this, almost all anarchist historians and scholars, from the very outset, point out that

Anarchist graffiti in Greece referred to the country's financial troubles in 2010. It says, "To get through the crisis we must sacrifice the bosses."

...α να ξεπεράσουμε ΚΡΙΣΗ πρέπει να Θυσιάσουμε ...τα ΑΦΕΝΤΙΚΑ

anarchism does not have to mean disorder and violence, but that it describes an alternative and holistic way to structure society. But anarchists as a group, let alone intellectuals who are sympathetic to anarchism, remain a very small minority, and it is no small task to change the accepted connotation of the word.

Alive in Action, Not Name

Anarchist communities exist today in Europe, particularly Belgium, and the movement is active in Greece. Although these communities self-identify as anarchist, many social reformers, including some prominent thinkers, are anarchist in action rather than name. This likely comes from a combination of factors. First of all, anarchism has consistently emphasized direct action—creating the ideal society in the present—over theories or ideas. Second, the negative associations with the word have proven hard to shake. Rather than anarchism, some follow twentieth-century French scholar Daniel Guérin, who used anarchism interchangeably with libertarian socialism as early as the 1960s. Libertarian socialism means the same thing as anarchism and should not be confused with libertarianism, a politically conservative position that emphasizes the sole authority of a free market. Third, and perhaps most important, many people who strive for equality, interdependence, mutual aid, and self-determination choose not to identify with any particular name or group.

Capitalism, a Common Foe

The majority of reformers across the globe who identify with traditionally anarchist principles today share a common foe: global capitalism. These reformers see the economic system as the greatest threat to nonhierarchical, egalitarian, community-based life. Of course, these individuals—particularly those of an anarchistic leaning—have any number of points of view. Some hold the traditionally anarchist anti-government stance, but what the vast majority share is a recognition that capitalism, and the system of class warfare and economic subjugation it engenders, is the greatest threat to a holistic and sustainable lifestyle for all.

NEW CHRISTIANA, ANARCHIST COMMUNITY

In 1971, a group of Danish progressives climbed the fences of an abandoned military compound and made it their home. Since then, more people moved into the area that has been referred to by various writers and members as an anarchist community, a free town, and a social experiment. This autonomous area of Copenhagen, Denmark, goes by New Christiana, or Free Town, and is home to roughly 1,000 people. Rent is paid to the community, and restaurants and shops are mutually owned. A college student visiting Free Town commented on the clean streets and the overwhelmingly friendly people. Critics have maintained that the lawless area is a haven for drugs. Free Town's status has been shaky since a law passed in 2004 allowing new development on the land.

Numerous leading intellectuals and activists have spoken out against the dangers of global capitalism. Some of these have anarchist roots or leanings. As early as 1952, Bookchin began warning of the dangers worldwide capitalism would place on human relationships and life—from food to community, natural resources, health, creativity, and happiness. Bookchin said, "Capitalism is a social cancer. It is the disease of society."[1]

Another leading critic of capitalism, Chomsky, has referred to corporations—the large companies that flourish in capitalism—as tyrannies. The goal of corporations is to increase profits, not to support the public good. In a 2000 interview with readers of the *Washington Post*, Chomsky said of corporations,

> *They have some latitude for public relations purposes, and the talk about corporate responsibility falls within that territory. But it makes no sense to regard them as benevolent institutions, freed from their institutional role. It is a public responsibility to enforce decent behavior.*[3]

"I've entertained many social theories which have a liberating effect on the restrictions that people have been living under. But I've never embraced any of them. I never could accept a doctrine that has definite boundaries to it. I just have to keep my mind free. The anarchists of all of them come closest to removing these restraints."[2]

—*Roger N. Baldwin, founder of the American Civil Liberties Union*

Critiques of global capitalism by leftist intellectuals gained a wider audience with the economic collapse of international markets of 2008. As the financial-market collapse made headlines, more and more people became aware of the inequity inherent in free markets. The subsequent calls for financial reform echoed concerns voiced by activists and thinkers, many with anarchist leanings, for decades.

Contemporary Solutions with Anarchist Roots

Many of the proposed solutions for the world-wide financial crisis and the climate crisis are reminiscent of anarchists' ideas. For example, the solutions Bookchin suggested through writing, teaching, and activism focused on building sustainable communities and moving toward localized, rather than centralized, control.

In connecting the expansion of capitalism with environmental catastrophe, Bookchin's work influenced a generation of activists and reformers who equate problems—including climate crisis, poverty, food and water shortages, labor injustice, and other social and environmental problems—with the rise of global capitalism. But Bookchin was critical of over-simplifying the problems and the solution; the change he promoted was wider in scale and more radical in scope. It included an active shift in thinking and behavior to create a more harmonious and less imbalanced society.

Today, green activists and social ecologists continue to push for local control of community and industry rather than global control. But large-scale change takes time, and contemporary activists, like many anarchists of the nineteenth and twentieth centuries, assert that the transition begins with small changes in behavior and thinking. For example, choosing to buy food at a farmers' market instead of a corporate grocery chain is one small step toward supporting local farm communities, decreasing pollution caused by industrial farming, and rethinking the impact individual choices have on the larger community.

On a larger scale, social ecologists advocate rethinking current solutions to the climate crisis. Instead of focusing on incentives for corporations to lessen practices and technologies that are harmful to the environment and to communities, they want to move toward more radical changes in societal and economic structures that empower people and communities around the world to live in more sustainable and holistic ways.

"The social problems we face—in politics, economics, gender and ethnic relations, and ecology—are not simply unrelated 'single issues' that should be dealt with separately. Like so many socialists and social anarchists in the past, I contend that an anarchist theory and practice that addresses them must be coherent, anchoring seemingly disparate social problems in an analysis of the underlying social relations: capitalism and hierarchical society."[4]

—*Murray Bookchin, anarchist and social ecologist*

Sharing Resources

How people use and share available resources, both natural and technological, is a vital part of an egalitarian society. Two different examples of shared resources can be found in contemporary times, one in the United States and the other in Bolivia.

In the United States, one of the most important concerns of the beginning of the twenty-first century has been health-care reform. Many people believe its resolution could move the country toward a more equitable and holistic society. In the 2009 presidential elections, candidate Barack Obama responded to concerns over rising health-care costs and millions of uninsured Americans by advocating for affordable health care for all. After he was elected president, Obama's administration drafted legislation to try to alleviate injustice and unnecessary expense in the health-care system. In March 2010, after a tempestuous national and legislative debate, President Obama signed an overhaul of the US health-care system into law.

Neither the solutions nor the means to addressing health-care reform are anarchist in a traditional sense. After all, it was the leader of government pushing for change, and the government that brought it into being will administer it. Because of this, however, conservative critics leveled the charge of socialism at health-care reform advocates, including the president. And critics on the left did not see the bill as going far enough toward equity.

What the ongoing health-care reform debate can illustrate is not decentralization but a movement toward eradicating one important form of class discrimination. In the present capitalist health-care system in the United States, many people believe the wealthy receive better care. In a new reformed system, people hope the poor and working classes are also guaranteed care. This shift represents evolution toward nonhierarchical and egalitarian, although not nongovernmental, society.

DOCUMENTARY OF CAPITALISM

In 2009, US documentary filmmaker Michael Moore released the movie *Capitalism, A Love Story,* which explores how corporate domination of the economy adversely affects US lives. Moore visited with many people who have lost their jobs, homes, or health insurance due to corporate practices that value profits over people.

A different approach to shared resources is seen in Bolivia, where President Evo Morales has resisted foreign investment in the country's natural resources. Bolivia is home to the world's largest known expanse of salt deposits, which are used to make lithium for batteries. As corporations seek to develop and market electric cars, lithium has become an increasingly valuable resource, one that Morales contends belongs equally to all citizens of Bolivia.

Rather than risk exploitation by foreign investors, Morales's government is developing plans and technology to extract the salt on their own and sell it for the benefit of the country. Though, like health-care reform, the Bolivian salt extraction project is government-run, its goal and methodology have the public interest in mind. It will expand public wealth through a process of mutual ownership and cooperation. In addition to enriching the country, the project has the potential to provide the kind of labor and collective ownership that anarcho-syndicalism advocates.

Online Freedom

The Internet is one of the most profound and contemporary examples of anarchism. Similar to contemporary activists and thinkers, however, it is not normally referred to as anarchist in name. Organizationally, there is no centralized power that controls the Internet. In place of that are a series of autonomous individuals, communities, social groups, and news media that interact, interrelate, and commonly share the resource.

But the freedom of the Internet is fragile. Corporations and some governments are trying to change it. There is no single governing body on the Internet, but some individual groups and governments do, at times, restrict the Internet. For example, in China, citizens are denied access to social networking and other Web sites that the government sees as harmful. Many people oppose these actions. Speaking to students in China about Internet freedom, President Obama said, "The more freely information flows, the stronger the society becomes, because then citizens of countries around the world can hold their own governments accountable."[5] Having an open structure for the Internet's web of information gives individuals freedom to articulate their views without fear of punishment.

Those against Internet freedom want to take control of this valuable resource and impose a centralized authority. In the case of the Internet, it is not only leftists or radical activists who step up to the fight. A wide spectrum of people strive to maintain Internet freedom.

One organization, The Internet Freedom Coalition, is dedicated to preserving the openness of the Internet. Its Web site states, "The Internet has become a powerful communications and economic force because it has been free from government interference."[6] Like anarchists before it, the group sees the lack of government authority as what makes the resource rich and sustaining for everyone.

WikiLeaks

The contemporary Web-based WikiLeaks represents a dramatic and effective example of anarchist ideals, principles, and organization. Started in 2007 by Australian Julian Assange, WikiLeaks is composed of autonomous individuals and collectives around the world that work together to achieve the goal of alleviating secrecy and promoting transparency in the media and governments. People around the world can anonymously submit information, and WikiLeaks publishes it. The Web site states, "WikiLeaks is a multi-jurisdictional public service designed to protect whistleblowers, journalists and activists who have sensitive materials to communicate to the public."[7]

WikiLeaks is structured similarly to an anarchist community. The engineers, activists, and journalists who participate in WikiLeaks do so on an almost exclusively voluntary basis and believe in the Web site's purpose. Centralized authority is replaced by organized participation that ensures each step of the complicated and sensitive job of disseminating information is done accurately.

The group also shares with anarchism an opposition to the bureaucracy and insularity of institutional governments. Founded in an era in which large corporations with the primary goal of profit, not news, are increasingly running media organizations, WikiLeaks is an active critique of capitalism and centralization of power.

DETAILING THE NEGATIVE ASPECTS OF CAPITALISM

In 2007, the critique of capitalism, widely promoted by intellectuals on the left, gained a wide audience through the work of Canadian author and activist Naomi Klein. Her book, *The Shock Doctrine: The Rise of Disaster Capitalism,* articulates in great detail the many ways that privatization and free trade have wreaked havoc on the economies and populations of people around the world. Klein's message hit home for many readers; her book made it to the *New York Times'* best-seller list and similar lists in ten countries.

Julian Assange is the founder of WikiLeaks, an online site structured like an anarchist community.

In subverting traditional lines of information protection around governments and corporations, WikiLeaks decreases government's and corporation's power of information and propaganda. Its patently antiauthoritarian stance against all forms of coercion has distinct anarchist roots. In response to a legal threat from the Church of Scientology, WikiLeaks posted this message on its site,

> WikiLeaks will not comply with legally abusive requests from Scientology any more than WikiLeaks has complied with similar demands from Swiss banks, Russian offshore stem-cell centers, former African kleptocrats, or the Pentagon.[8] ⌘

12

Reality or Utopia?

In addition to anarchism's tendency toward violence, one primary concern critics level at anarchism is that its ideals are not realistic and instead represent a utopia. But anarchists have consistently maintained that the society they suggest is not a dream but a realistic possibility. Perhaps because of this criticism, anarchists have always insisted that change begins with direct action in the present. Although direct action has been interpreted by some to be a violent or aggressive act, to the vast majority of anarchists, it means changing one's attitude and behavior to be consistent with one's principles, not with the powers that be.

Some people believe the kind of society anarchists protest for is an unattainable utopia.

As many scholars and activists have noted, there is no single doctrine or prescribed set of rules that define anarchism. Anarchist historian Rudolf Rocker summed up this perspective, writing that anarchism is not

> a fixed, self-enclosed social system but rather a definite trend in the historic development of mankind, which, in contrast with the intellectual guardianship of all clerical and governmental institutions, strives for the free, unhindered unfolding of all the individual and social forces in life.[1]

As contemporary history proves, this trend toward individual freedom and away from exploitation can function under a variety of names. In the original anarchist formulation, it included abolishing the state, and many anarchists still believe in this. Others, perhaps the greater majority, see the most problematic source of authority today as economic and cite capitalism as the great menace to freedom and equality. Regardless of the source of authority or how the fight is conducted, anarchism has provided a way to rethink and remake society. Anarchists' greatest contribution has been to imagine—and to set into motion—a society free of coercion or exploitation with shared resources and liberties.

Social Evolution

Some believe that anarchism is the direction in which society is moving. Herbert Read echoes the thoughts of anarchists before and after him:

> The essential principle of anarchism is that mankind has reached a stage of development at which it is possible to abolish the old relationship of master-man (capitalist-proletarian) and substitute a relationship of egalitarian co-operation.[2]

From Kropotkin to Rocker to Guerín to Chomsky, anarchist thinkers and sympathizers have supported the idea that the society they envision is a natural outcome of societal growth. Although some scholars have seen anarchism as a side note to Marxism, anarchist scholars note that Marx himself saw anarchism as a different embodiment of his ideas.

Today, there are subgroups of anarchists who believe that technology has further eroded culture and that people should return to a primitive state. But the larger body of progressive thinkers sees this as a regression backward. Technology, as Chomsky pointed out, "is a pretty neutral instrument."[3] Regarding technology as a force for social change, Chomsky continued,

> Technology could in fact be used to help the workforce in a factory run [the factory] without any managers, by providing people at the workbench real-time information that would enable them to join with others in making sensible decisions.[4]

Even a contemporary industrialized and highly technological society could harness these tools as a means for reorganizing labor and relationships to put power in the hands of the people.

An analysis of history could support the anarchist point of view that humans are moving toward the society they project, that the revolution anarchists have dreamed about may actually be composed of the evolution of humankind. In the United States, people have progressively gained more freedoms and individual liberties. Throughout the twentieth century, most of Europe moved into more socially just configurations, making health care and other resources available to all. In general, the majority of societies across the globe steadily promote more independence and freedom.

Template for Anarchism

Another challenge for anarchists has been to make the society they envision a reality to others. Humans have adopted a long-term habit of authority, and for many people, conceiving of a society without government is frightening and seems impossible. Because of this, many anarchists—from Kropotkin

VIOLENT ANARCHISTS STILL TARNISH NAME

Although proponents believe anarchism has outgrown violence, isolated examples continue to plague the movement. During the 2001 protests against the World Bank and International Monetary Fund in Seattle, Washington, large, peaceful protests were thrown off kilter by the aggression of a few self-declared anarchists. In this way, the violent strain of anarchism is perpetuated while the predominant and peaceful strain is often misrepresented or adopts another name.

to Argentine economist Diego Abad de Santillán and Russian-American Alexander Berkman—have sketched out how an anarchist society would function.

These proposals for anarchist society vary in detail and depth, but in some form, they share individual and communal control at a local level. The basic idea is that groups of laborers, craftspeople, or intellectuals would comprise collectives that share a common purpose and collaborate to share resources and information and ensure that the work of their group gets done. These smaller groups would then communicate and interrelate with a larger group and with other collectives. The same would take place in neighborhoods.

For a simple example, a group of economics professors could form a collective. They would meet when necessary to discuss goals, share research, and ensure that economics students are getting the information and assistance they need. This group would then communicate with and meet, though less regularly, with a larger body of economics professors, nationally or internationally, as well as with professors of other disciplines who live in the same local community. In this way, professors would self-organize their administrative and professional duties and needs.

This same structure would take place in communities so that a council would meet to take care of what is needed in any given local community and delegates would collaborate with councils in the larger area, nationally and internationally. This structure is similar in principle to democracy, and still seems a bit hierarchical, but what anarchism supports is a more direct form of structure and communication that begins and ends with the people. In this scenario, authority is not handed down from the leaders at the top, but delegated by and among the people themselves. Rather than elected leaders, everyone in a community would take turns participating in administrative and other areas.

Individuals would have the freedom to do whatever job they were inclined to do. No single job would be more valuable than another, and all would receive equal pay, whether in the form of money, benefits, resources, or a combination of these. Since individuals would choose the way they want to grow, develop, and work, they would have a greater investment in their jobs, which would result in a more harmonious and productive society. If there were tasks no one wanted to do, community members would take turns and share that work equally.

Deep Change

The change anarchists promote involves a shift in humans' interactions with one another and the environment that would ultimately dismantle destructive systems—economic, governmental, or otherwise—and replace them with more holistic ones. They assert that it requires a shift in minds and habits, including recognizing and understanding the subtle and overt ways that advertising, public relations, the free market, wage-labor, and other aspects of capitalism and government control emotions and behavior.

Furthermore, it would require far greater investment and participation in the daily workings of society.

Anarchists and leftists often place the blame of limited participation in society on the centralization of a government that they see as operating from the top down. If this were flipped, so that people had a say in their daily lives, participation would increase. As early as the 1950s, Herbert Read cited the low percentage of citizens who exercise their right to vote, seeing this as a failure of the democratic system:

> "There has never been an anarchist movement. There were isolated groups and sects that often quarreled with each other, each one going its own way. It is a philosophy taking many different forms. But they all agree on freedom of expression and resistance to controls by one person over another. It never was born and never will die. For it springs from the human soul and will last as long as man lasts."[7]
>
> —*Roger N. Baldwin, founder of American Civil Liberties Union*

> If you go into a village and propose to introduce electric power; if you go into a city street and propose to widen it . . . then you touch the immediate interests of the citizen. Put these questions to the voter and without any coaxing or canvassing, he will run to the polls.[5]

Read's conclusion still resonates today: "In short, real politics are local politics."[6]

More recently, Chomsky was asked to explain his position on voting. He emphasized his participation in local elections, issues that directly affect him and his community, over national elections, in which he participates only when his vote will have an impact—for example, in a swing state. This is opposed to the common viewpoint that every vote makes a difference. More optimistic than Read about real possibilities for change, Chomsky cites the numerous progressive social changes and individual freedoms people have sought—and gained—over the past century.

The Anarchist Dilemma

One of the biggest divides that anarchists and others on the left of the political spectrum have faced is how to achieve the kind of revolutionary change they seek. In earlier times, the question was one of whether the revolution would be fast, violent, and radical, or slow, gradual, and sustainable. But today, most anarchist thinkers believe the movement has outgrown violence. The pacifist anarchism of Tolstoy or Landauer was echoed by the nonviolent resistance of important twentieth-century figures for change including Martin Luther King Jr. in the United States, Mohandas Gandhi in India, and Nelson Mandela in South Africa. The question now has become one of compromise: How much can an anarchist, or activist, participate in government and still criticize it?

This question divided early anarchists and continues to elicit several answers today. Proudhon opposed all forms of coercion, authority, and violence and yet served for a brief time in the National Assembly. Historian Richard Sonn wrote, "Proudhon bequeathed to anarchism a positive program, which unfortunately would be overshadowed by the violent revolutionary negation of Mikhail Bakunin."[8] But today, more than a century later, Proudhon's more gradual change dominates the progressive agenda. His ideas live on in credit unions, interdependent cyberspace, local farming, and many other community-centered cultural and economic changes. Birgitta Jonsdottir, an artist, poet, activist, and member of WikiLeaks, provided a contemporary example of active, conscious participation. Elected to the Icelandic Parliament in 2009, Jonsdottir said,

> When we first got to parliament, the staff was so nervous: here are people who were protesting parliament, who were for revolution, and now we are inside. None of us had aspirations to be politicians. We have a checklist, and, once we're done, we are out.[9]

Like Jonsdottir, the goal for many activists today is to participate in government to the extent that it makes a difference in shifting society toward increased equality, access to resources, and independence in lifestyle, cultural, and economic choices.

How to Proceed

During the 1930s, at the tail end of the heyday of anarchism, publications attempted to bring young people into the movement. Many early

American anarchists were immigrants, with cultural and philosophical roots in other countries. As they aged, their children were more grounded in American culture. Like many young people, they were mostly uninterested in what they saw as the old ideas of their parents and grandparents. Anarchism, small as it was to begin with, largely went out of fashion.

Despite isolated anarchist communities, and even international anarchist organizations, by most standards, anarchism has little overt impact on today's world. And yet, the ideals it stands for, and the direction it points, are more prominent now than ever.

In today's complex global culture, it is difficult to know whether anarchism will have the same revolutionary appeal as it did in the past century. This is perhaps due to its insistence on deep change, a greater threat to the dominant order than the flagrant antiauthoritarianism in empty rebellion. Capitalism, the dominant economic system in the world today, has a way of consuming and taming rebellious social and cultural trends. For example, punk rock was once a rebellious attack on corporate culture, but now its styles and ideas are widely accepted and marketed as a fashion style.

Still, the principles that anarchism stands for, and the society it imagines, are in greater reach today than at any other time in history. More people are realistically recognizing and honestly assessing capitalism, finding that it can manipulate and assert authority over work, relationships, food, health, and other vital areas of life. More

Capitalism can tame rebellious social trends, such as punk rock, which has spread around the world.

people may begin to make different choices that will continue the gradual movement away from increased authority and toward the society anarchists imagine, made up of empowered individuals and autonomous local communities. ⌘

Quick Facts

Definition of Anarchism

Anarchism is a social, cultural, political, and economic belief and way of life that sees the state as unnecessary and undesirable and advocates for a society without hierarchy based on mutual cooperation, co-ownership of resources, and voluntary participation.

Well-Known Anarchist Countries

No anarchist countries currently exist because anarchists are against state formation. However, anarchism has played an active role in numerous European and Latin American countries from the late 1880s through the early 1920s. Specifically, anarchism was prominent in Spain from the early twentieth century until the end of the Spanish Civil War in 1939. Also, Ukraine was briefly anarchist in 1919. Anarchist pockets continue today in Europe, particularly in Belgium.

Organization of Anarchism

Anarchists have designed and specified various possibilities for organization, most of which include local organization into autonomous communities or collaborative groups that would then interact with other local groups and similar collectives internationally. Rather than elected officials, people would alternate to hold positions in decision-making groups.

Main Leadership Position

There is no head of state or leader in an anarchist society. Anarchists believe in equality and do not believe any single person is more important or valuable than another. Anarchist societies are based on nonhierarchical structures, without titles or salaries.

Founders and Advocates

French philosopher and activist Pierre-Joseph Proudhon and Russian activist Mikhail Bakunin are the primary founders of anarchism. Proudhon wrote many books on anarchism, including his first and best-known book, *What Is Property?*, published in 1840, and also served briefly in the National Assembly. He promoted a form of gradual and peaceful change rather than violent means. Bakunin, the more incendiary of the leaders, advocated for revolutionary change in any way possible. He played an important role in the early founding of the International Working Men's Association and founded an anarchist version of the association that proved active in Spain, Switzerland, Belgium, and Latin America.

Historic Leaders

Other important voices in the history of anarchism include Peter Kropotkin, Nestor Makhno, Emma Goldman, and Alexander Berkman. Kropotkin was the author of numerous texts on anarchism, including his most famous work, *Fields, Factories, and Workshops*, published in 1912. Makhno led an anarchist army in Ukraine during the Russian Revolution, successfully claiming Ukraine for anarchists for a few months in 1919. Goldman gave numerous rousing speeches, speaking out for workers' rights, women's health, and equality for all. Berkman was active in the anarchist movement in the United States.

How Power Shifts

Since the nineteenth century, there has been a debate among anarchist philosophers about whether anarchism should be achieved through a gradual shift in power from the government to the people, as Proudhon advocated, or through a violent overthrow or revolution, as Bakunin promoted.

Economic Systems

There are two primary ideas about economics in anarchism. The better known of these is syndicalism, which mirrors communism, in that workers are organized into collectives that mutually co-own the means of production. The second idea retains individual property, such as artisans owning their own crafts, but promotes free trade and zero-interest loans and is against capital. In all anarchist communities, labor is equivalent, and no job or role is more valued than another. For most anarchists, money should be replaced by trade.

The Roles of Citizens

Because anarchism is against government by the few, individual citizens play a vital role in the healthy functioning of anarchist societies. Individual citizens are voluntary members of autonomous communities that self-govern, so people take turns being part of decision-making bodies. In addition, members of communities co-own resources and all take part in the work of the community, participating as they choose. All citizens equally share the tasks no one wants to do.

Personal Freedoms and Rights

Above all else, anarchism values individual freedom and independence for all members of a community, where all resources are shared. This includes providing all citizens with what they need to thrive, including work, shelter, food, and freedom of thought and belief. Anarchistic ideas of liberty are holistic and integrate the importance of leisure, art, and spirituality along with meeting basic needs.

Strengths of Anarchism

- Flexibility
- Equality
- Liberty
- No hierarchy
- Choice in work, education, and religion
- Value placed on art and spirituality
- Functions in harmony with community and environment

Weaknesses of Anarchism

- Freedom of choice for all makes organization challenging.
- Relative to traditional forms of government, it has not survived as an organizing principle for large amounts of people for long stretches of time.
- A major shift in society's thinking patterns and organization is required.
- Individuals have elected to achieve change through violence.

Glossary

adherent
Someone who believes in, or is associated with, a particular set of beliefs.

authoritarianism
A system of government with power concentrated in a small group or a single individual.

bureaucracy
An administrative system characterized by specialized groups, fixed rules, and hierarchy.

capital
Accumulated goods, especially money.

capitalism
An economic system in which individuals or corporations control capital, and prices for goods and services are determined by competition in the free market.

centralization
The placement of power or authority in a single, central organization.

collective
A cooperative group.

communism
The economic and political system based on collective ownership of property and equal distribution of goods.

doctrine
A principle or position, usually a foundational governmental or religious law.

equity
Justice according to a natural law that is free of bias.

exploitation
Using a person or resources for unfair gain or advantage.

fascism
A political philosophy that exalts the leader or a group of people over the individual; characterized by dictatorial rule, oppression, and the forceful stopping of resistance.

leftist
Supporting the political views of the left.

liberal
Open to new behavior and not bound by traditional values.

Marxism
A form of socialism outlined by Karl Marx that advocates for a period of dictatorship over the proletariat, or workers, en route to the establishment of a classless society.

monarchy
A form of government led by a king or a queen.

nonhierarchical
A structure in which there are no levels or classes, where people are equal and classless.

propaganda
Information intended to mislead or influence and promote a particular political cause or point of view.

revolution
Forcible overthrow of a government or social order in favor of a new system.

socialism
An economic system based on collective or state ownership of industry and business.

subjugate
To bring a subject under control and governance.

sustainable
Relating to a method that does not permanently deplete resources.

Additional Resources

Selected Bibliography

Avrich, Paul. *Anarchist Voices: An Oral History of Anarchism in America*. Princeton, NJ: Princeton UP, 1995. Print.

Baldwin, Roger, ed. *Anarchism: A Collection of Revolutionary Writings*. New York: Dover, 2002. Print.

Chomsky, Noam. *Chomsky on Anarchism*. Oakland, CA: AK, 2005. Print.

Fellner, Gene. *Life of an Anarchist: The Alexander Berkman Reader*. New York: Seven Stories, 1992. Print.

Read, Herbert. *Anarchy and Order: Essays in Politics*. Boston: Beacon, 1971. Print.

Sonn, Richard D. *Anarchism*. New York: Twayne, 1992. Print.

Further Readings

Bamyeh, Mohammed A. *Anarchy as Order: The History and Future of Civic Humanity*. Lanham, MD: Rowman, 2009. Print.

Kahn, Richard. *Contemporary Anarchist Studies: An Introductory Anthology of Anarchy in the Academy*. New York: Routledge, 2009. Print.

Kropotkin, Peter. *Anarchism: A Collection of Revolutionary Writings*. Mineola, NY: Dover, 2002. Print.

Web Links

To learn more about anarchism, visit ABDO Publishing Company online at **www.abdopublishing.com.** Web sites about anarchism are featured on our Book Links page. These links are routinely monitored and updated to provide the most current information available.

Places to Visit

Gazebo for Emma Goldman
Public Sculpture at Beloit College
700 College Street, Beloit, WI, 53511
This steel sculpture was created by artist and anarchist Siah Armajani in commemoration of Emma Goldman.

Haymarket Memorial
Desplaines Street and Lake Street, Chicago, IL 60607
The public sculpture by artist Mary Brogger commemorates the eight anarchists who died during the tragedy at Haymarket Square in 1889.

Sacco and Vanzetti Memorial
Community Church of Boston
565 Boylston Street in Copley Square, Boston, MA 02116
617-266-6710
www.communitychurchofboston.org
This bronze plaque of Italian-American anarchists Nicola Sacco and Bartolomeo Vanzetti honors the men many believe were wrongly convicted of robbery and executed by the state of Massachusetts. Gutzon Borglum, the same artist who designed the Mount Rushmore presidential sculpture in South Dakota, created the memorial.

Source Notes

Chapter 1. What Is Anarchism?

1. Gene Fellner. *Life of an Anarchist: The Alexander Berkman Reader*. New York: Seven Stories, 1992. Print. 268.

2. "Anarchy." *Merriam-Webster*. Merriam-Webster, Inc., 2010. Web. 23 Sept. 2010.

3. Herbert Read. *Anarchy and Order: Essays in Politics*. Boston: Beacon, 1971. Print. 117.

4. Gene Fellner. *Life of an Anarchist: The Alexander Berkman Reader*. New York: Seven Stories, 1992. Print. Forward.

5. Herbert Read. *Anarchy and Order: Essays in Politics*. Boston: Beacon, 1971. Print. ix.

Chapter 2. Early History of Anarchism

1. Peter Kropotkin. *A Collection of Revolutionary Writings*. Mineola, NY: Dover, 2002. Print. 290.

2. Richard D. Sonn. *Anarchism*. New York: Twayne, 1992. Print. 27.

3. Ibid. 28.

4. Ann Robertson. "The Philosophical Roots of the Marx-Bakunin Conflict." *Marxists Internet Archives*. N.p, Dec. 2003. Web. 23 Sept. 2010.

5. Ibid.

6. Daniel Guérin. *Anarchism: From Theory to Practice*. New York: Monthly Review, 1970. Print. 15.

Chapter 3. The Heyday Part One: Anarchism and Violence

1. Richard D. Sonn. *Anarchism*. New York: Twayne, 1992. Print. 36.

2. "Haymarket and May Day." *Electronic Encyclopedia of Chicago*. Chicago Historical Society, 2005. Web. 23 Sept. 2010.

3. Ibid.

Chapter 4. The Heyday Part Two: Anarchism and Society

1. Richard D. Sonn. *Anarchism*. New York: Twayne, 1992. Print. 47.

2. Candace Falk, ed. *Emma Goldman: A Documentary History of the American Years*. Berkeley, CA: U of California P, 2003. Print. 288.

3. Ibid. 289.

Chapter 5. Poetry, Protest, and Punks

1. Herbert Read. *Anarchy and Order: Essays in Politics*. Boston: Beacon, 1971. Print. 88.

2. Richard D. Sonn. *Anarchism*. New York: Twayne, 1992. Print. 104.

3. Ibid.

Chapter 6. Anarchism and Revolution

1. Howard Zinn. Introduction. *Anarchy & Order*. By Herbert Read. Boston: Beacon, 1971. Print. xviii.

2. Gene Fellner, ed. *Life of an Anarchist: The Alexander Berkman Reader*. New York: Seven Stories, 1992. Print. 281.

3. Herbert Read. *Anarchy and Order: Essays in Politics*. Boston: Beacon, 1971. Print. 51.

4. Noam Chomsky. *Chomsky on Anarchism*. Oakland, CA: AK, 2005. Print. 234.

5. Roger Baldwin, ed. *Anarchism: A Collection of Revolutionary Writings*. New York: Dover, 2002. Print. 35.

6. Judith Suissa. "Anarchy in the Classroom." *New Humanist* 120.5, Sept./Oct. 2005. *NewHumanist.org.uk*. The Rationalist Association, n.d. Web. 23 Sept. 2010.

7. Noam Chomsky. *Chomsky on Anarchism*. Oakland, CA: AK, 2005. Print. 222.

8. Richard D. Sonn. *Anarchism*. New York: Twayne, 1992. Print. 43.

Chapter 7. Anarchist Economics

1. Gene Fellner, ed. *Life of an Anarchist: The Alexander Berkman Reader*. New York: Seven Stories, 1992. Print. 281.
2. Ibid.
3. Noam Chomsky. *Chomsky on Anarchism*. Oakland, CA: AK, 2005. Print. 120.

Chapter 8. Anarchism and Art

1. Howard Zinn. Introduction. *Anarchy & Order*. By Herbert Read. Boston: Beacon, 1971. Print. x.
2. Herbert Read. *Anarchy and Order: Essays in Politics*. Boston: Beacon, 1971. Print. 63.
3. Ibid.
4. Richard D. Sonn. *Anarchism*. New York: Twayne, 1992. Print. 52.
5. Herbert Read. *Anarchy and Order: Essays in Politics*. Boston: Beacon, 1971. Print. 67.
6. Tristan Tzara. "Dadaism." *University of Pennsylvania*. James F. English, n.d. Web. 23 Sept. 2010.

Chapter 9. Forms of Anarchism

1. Noam Chomsky. *Chomsky on Anarchism*. Oakland, CA: AK, 2005. Print. 118.
2. Ibid. 123.
3. Tom Powdrill. "Murray Bookchin Quote on Capitalism." *Labour and Capital*. Tom Powdrill, 13 Oct. 2007. Web. 23 Sept. 2010.
4. "About the ISE." Institute for Social Ecology Online. *Institute for Social Ecology*, 2 Mar. 1998. Web. 23 Sept. 2010.

Chapter 10. Case Studies

1. Richard D. Sonn. *Anarchism*. New York: Twayne, 1992. Print. 70.
2. "Nestor Makho." *The Anarchist Encyclopedia: A Gallery of Saints & Sinners*. N.p., Sept. 2009. Web. 23 Sept. 2010.

3. Paul Avrich. *Anarchist Voices: An Oral History of Anarchism in America.* Princeton, NJ: Princeton UP, 1995. Print. 65.

4. Noam Chomsky. *Chomsky on Anarchism.* Oakland, CA: AK, 2005. Print. 135.

Chapter 11. An Anarchist Legacy

1. Mike Small. "Murray Bookchin: US political thinker whose ideas shaped the anti-globalisation movement." *Guardian.co.uk.* Guardian News and Media Limited, 8 Aug. 2006. Web. 23 Sept. 2010.

2. Paul Avrich. *Anarchist Voices: An Oral History of Anarchism in America.* Princeton, NJ: Princeton UP, 1995. Print. 64.

3. "Globalization and Its Discontents: Noam Chomsky debates with Washington Post readers." *Washington Post.* 16 May 2000. *Chomsky.info.* N.p., n.d. Web. 23 Sept. 2010.

4. Murray Bookchin. "Whither Anarchism? A Reply to Recent Anarchist Critics." Institute for Social Ecology Online. *Institute for Social Ecology*, 2 Mar. 1998. Web. 23 Sept. 2010.

5. Mary Papenfuss. "Obama Nudges China on Internet Freedom: Openness Makes Nations Stronger, President Tells Students." *Newser.com.* Newser LLC, 16 Nov. 2009. Web. 23 Sept. 2010.

6. "About Us." *Internetfreedomcoalition.org.* Internet Freedom Coalition, N.d. Web. 23 Sept. 2010.

7. "WikiLeaks: About." *Wikileaks.org.* Sunshine, N.d. Web. 23 Sept. 2010.

8. Raffi Khatchadourian. "No Secrets: Julian Assange's mission for total transparency." *The New Yorker* 7 June 2010. *The New Yorker.* Condé Nast Digital, n.d. Web. 23 Sept. 2010.

Chapter 12. Reality or Utopia?

1. Noam Chomsky. *Chomsky on Anarchism.* Oakland, CA: AK, 2005. Print. 118.

2. Herbert Read. *Anarchy and Order: Essays in Politics.* Boston: Beacon, 1971. Print. 92.

3. Noam Chomsky. *Chomsky on Anarchism*. Oakland, CA: AK, 2005. Print. 225.

4. Ibid.

5. Herbert Read. *Anarchy and Order: Essays in Politics*. Boston: Beacon, 1971. Print. 105.

6. Ibid.

7. Paul Avrich. *Anarchist Voices: An Oral History of Anarchism in America*. Princeton, NJ: Princeton UP, 1995. Print. 65.

8. Richard D. Sonn. *Anarchism*. New York: Twayne, 1992. Print. 27.

9. Raffi Khatchadourian. "No Secrets: Julian Assange's mission for total transparency." *The New Yorker* 7 June 2010. *The New Yorker*. Condé Nast Digital, n.d. Web. 23 Sept. 2010.

Index